Owner Unknown

Your Guide to
Real Estate
Treasure Hunting

by J. D. Segel

GENEALOGICAL PUBLISHING Co. Inc.

Dust jacket designed by Edward L. Downes

Contents

This book is dedicated to
my wife, Shelly, and my son, Kevin,
whose love and support are my main assets.

Preface

This book invites you on a journey that requires you to bring only your creative instincts, organizational skills, patience, and perseverance. A working knowledge of genealogy and local events, both past and present, will help but is not mandatory. Together we will explore and unravel the mysteries of the last frontier in real estate, and in the process provide you an opportunity to reap untold personal and financial rewards. Our subject: "owner unknown" land.

Parcels of untitled, untaxed land, of unknown ownership, exist in many states and are ripe for the taking. Inexperienced individuals such as yourself do clear these titles, develop these lands, and realize great profit and personal satisfaction—however, this book is not a get-rich-quick manual. For one thing, these projects require hard work, with no short cuts and no guarantee of success. Simply stated, the task requires finding a parcel of owner-unknown land, identifying a previous owner, determining the last known owner, tracing the heirs, and acquiring deeds to the tract from these heirs.

In the course of your investigation you will come up against what seem to be insurmountable obstacles, but don't let that throw you. Title to property passes by deed, death, or decree, so you can expect to encounter all sorts of unusual situations. The answers are out there somewhere; you just have to find them. If this was easy, somebody else would already have figured it out. You must be prepared for surprises, which often require imaginative responses and swift action. There will be many false starts and second guesses. Evidence will present itself at every turn, but you must sort out fact from fiction. Follow your hunches, because opportunities for action and discovery can disappear as suddenly as they surface.

The path to success has been carefully outlined between the covers of this book, which is designed both to help you and to motivate you. This volume should be viewed as a guide, not the gospel. It would be next to impossible to cover all the contingencies, conditions, and circumstances for every situation that one might encounter. My intent is to provide a practical and easy-to-use guide that introduces the subject and contains sufficient information to enable you to undertake your own quest.

The methods described here can also be used to trace your own ancestry. In fact, these two adventures may not be mutually exclusive. You may be an heir to a parcel of owner-unknown land or some other inheritance. There are literally billions of dollars in unclaimed assets, hidden in probate files, that belong to unsuspecting people just like you. In essence, this book is your guide to real estate treasure hunting, whether in your own backyard or far afield.

I remember hearing about the days when good old-fashioned enterprise and persistence would get you ahead, but it's not that easy anymore. I look at owner-unknown land as a wonderful opportunity where diligence, tenacity, and a commitment to project resolution can pay big dividends. The process can be tedious and packed with frustration, but few exercises promise as much of a payoff for both the ego and the pocketbook. If you feel your frustration-level peaking, think of this as an exciting educational experience or a challenging puzzle, and any financial return as found money. In any event the endeavor should offer fun and a sense of accomplishment. What a feeling of satisfaction to help a family fill in gaps in their history, to generate tax revenue for a town, or to establish a well-earned, real asset for yourself and your heirs! This book knows no boundaries.

With the advent of computer recordkeeping, fewer parcels of owner-unknown land are appearing, while existing lots in question are being claimed. You now stand in a window of opportunity that narrows each day. All owner-unknown parcels are owned by someone. These "someones" don't just vanish without leaving a trail, so it's up to you to find them. Whether you are a casual observer of life looking for an interesting challenge or an aggressive go-getter seeking a new outlet for your energies, or you are among those who simply relish a good detective story, this is an engraved invitation for you to take yourself on. Some people say that there are winners and losers, but I say there are winners and those waiting to win. This book is about empowering everyone to win by participating in a fascinating and richly fulfilling activity. Good luck, and don't take no for an answer!

Getting Started

As in most specialized fields, owner-unknown property research has its own set of technical terms. Precise understanding of this jargon is imperative for the uninitiated. Though modern legal terms and usage, as applied to real estate, are difficult enough for the novice to fully comprehend, the language and format in older documents can be bewildering, providing a formidable challenge to even the most savvy and experienced of title examiners. A selected glossary of terms and abbreviations has been provided in Appendix 8. This lexicon should be referred to any time you have the slightest doubt as to the meaning of a term. In deeds and wills, every word has the potential to change the flow and thereby the status of land. Should you miss an element of the progression, you may end up with deeds from uninterested parties and, technically, no rights to the parcel in question.

Consider at the outset whether you want to go the solo route or recruit partners or friends who might bring different areas of expertise to the project. The most successful groups seem to be multi-disciplinary and contain an archivist, a genealogist, a historian, and an able and insatiable researcher to perform the crucial spadework. Turn to Appendix 3, "Owner Unknown from A to Z," for a concise, step-by-step view of the process and you will get a better idea of the most suitable people for a team effort. Make sure that someone is responsible for every task on the flow chart and that there is a designated leader to set overall tempo and direction. Whether proceeding independently or in a group, a trip to the local office supply store will be necessary to pick up file folders, pens, pencils, highlighters, magnifying glasses, notebooks, tape, sketch pads, rulers, staplers, and other organizational and logistical tools.

The first and most critical decision you will make is where to search for owner-unknown parcels. As a rule of thumb owner-unknown lots are most prevalent in rural areas and near boundary lines. Pay special attention to areas just beyond the pale of present development. These scattered tracts are good targets for owner-unknown probes, ripe in that they are relatively unresearched, and yet they are likely at some point to attract prospective developers and thus have the potential for a dramatic increase in value. It will be advantageous, then, to examine demographic studies and statistics that show migration trends from saturated areas to the surrounding rural towns of a region. Population data can usually be derived from town, county, and state registers, or from maps and atlases. Census reports also contain relevant information and offer a broad perspective that I have found useful in my projects.

Whatever the specific circumstances leading to the unknown ownership status of the property, you can bet that the municipality is always at least partly responsible for the situation. In fact, an owner-unknown label is an official admission of carelessness, mismanagement, lack of effective oversight, or outright ineptitude by local authorities. At the root of the problem is a lack of communication. This usually exists on many levels, but it always involves the local tax collector, assessor, and the last known owner or his heirs. Their dereliction is your opportunity.

Many people have asked me why these municipalities don't just take the land in question. The local authorities are usually limited in these matters by state statutes protecting unknown heirs. To gain ownership the town essentially must follow the same methods put forth in this manual for title and heir searching, the only legal and effective mechanisms to ascertain the correct ownership of real property. The town can then purify the title with a proper tax-taking and any necessary court proceedings. However, this process can be time-consuming, because tax bills must be issued and the rightful heirs given a period in which to respond before any tax-taking can begin. Local authorities have seized so-called owner-unknown land without following the appropriate legal remedies and have lost in court because of their failure to properly close out the right of redemption vested in all interested parties. Municipalities do have another option, that of exercising the principle of eminent domain—but this is also a protracted proceeding and may be costly, since the town must agree, at a special meeting, to the taking of the land and to pay the fair market value.

At various points in your investigation you may encounter pockets of resistance, primarily from "townies"—local people with ties to their governing body or its records. I have found that a polite but firm and forthright manner, coupled with an expressed willingness to share certain information, will win these people over. It may take some time, but your patience, diligence, openness, and sincerity will earn their respect and tolerance.

Throughout the project you will need to examine and obtain copies of a wide variety of records. This right of access to public documents is protected by a federal statute known as the Freedom of Information Act. This law enables individuals to pursue genealogical and historical research in public records, but grants the right to public agencies to withhold access in certain instances in order to protect confidentiality, security, or privacy. At the local level, regulations governing the rights of privacy fall under the purview of the states, which have their own restrictions as to what records are accessible to whom, and when. Availability of a document from a tax assessment office or a bureau of wills, for example, may depend on the identity and relationship of the person requesting the information (whether he or she is a blood relative) or on other conditions, such as a specified lapse time for release of information. In most states official death records are not publicly available until 100 years after the decedent's death, but a surviving spouse or child can generally get a copy of the certificate whenever they want. A complete list of these statutes can be found in a publication called *A Summary of Freedom of Information and Privacy Laws of the 50 States* (obtainable from Plus Publications, Inc., 2626 Pennsylvania Ave., N.W., Washington, DC 20037). It is important to remember that these laws apply to documents held in government offices or repositories. The records you seek may be available from other private sources, such as the local historical society.

There are a number of other reference works you will find helpful, including books on history, research methodology, law, and genealogy. I have compiled a list of such items in Appendix 9. One of the best preparations for an owner-unknown research project, once you have decided on a locale, is to peruse local history books, which will acquaint you with the nature of the region and its settlers and subsequent residents. These histories range from full-length narratives to documentary collections, and experience has taught me that both types can be beneficial. Many states have conveyancers' handbooks that will familiarize you with local real estate law. These books have proven indispensable to me and are not as intimidating as you might think, as they are designed for use not only by attorneys, but also by their support staff and other non-professional interested parties. They are regularly updated and usually contain convenient forms such as deed, abstract, and declaration of trust boilerplates that you will need later in the process.

Finally, it is advisable to drive through the municipal area looking for neglected tracts of land and landmarks, making notes as you go. A hand-held micro-cassette recorder is a good choice for these spontaneous notations. If this area is not local to your residence, pick up a phonebook that contains listings for it. Appendix 2 is a blank organizational phone directory that, at completion, will contain most of the telephone numbers you will need.

Now, take a moment to glance at the rest of the appendices prepared for you in the back of this guide. Appendix 10 contains a catalog, organized by state, of selected repositories and other agencies that may aid you in the course of your search. Make a copy of the blank phone appendix and begin transferring the numbers from the state references appendix. Pull out that phonebook you procured on the scouting excursion and complete the phone list, then get to a phone and begin making contacts. You'll need to learn the hours, fees, procedures, and locations of these institutions. Ask to speak to the librarian, curator, clerk, or some other person of authority and introduce yourself as a researcher. This telephone introduction will usually make your initial visit more congenial and infinitely more constructive.

Town Hall

Y ou are now ready to choose a locus, or parcel of land—in our case a tract on which no one is currently paying a property tax and which is labeled as "owner unknown" in a local assessor's office. Choosing a locus launches the adventure. With my help and your application, this parcel will be your prize and pride at the end of a successful quest. The stage is set. You gain entry through the pages of an oversized real estate resource known as the "assessor's reference book." Many realtors have bound versions of this tome in their offices. However, for the most comprehensive and current owner information I advise you to go to the unbound geographical index, or field cards, located in the assessor's office, which, in most municipalities, you will find in or near the town hall.

In your notebook, label the top of page 1 "Owner-Unknown Parcels," and include the name of the town in which you are working. You may also wish to jot down the current date for later reference. Most assessor's books have three parts: maps, geographical index, and owner information. The "maps" part begins with a composite overview that permits broad visualization and easy reference by dividing the town into numbered sectors that correspond to more detailed maps that follow. The town assessor will assign a map and parcel number to every piece of land in the jurisdiction, unless it has been combined with another tract. This section will give you the location and physical description of your locus, as well as identifying its "abutters"—those who are paying property tax on the parcels of land next to your locus.

Abutters' names and addresses will be important when you begin researching the title to your parcel.

The geographical index usually contains a "parcel to owner" cross-reference system that matches map and parcel numbers with the corresponding lot numbers. This directory, which may also appear as a separate book or card file, is where you will find parcels of land designated variously as "owner unknown," "unknown owner," or "persons unknown." Diligently thumb through the book or cards and list all the parcels whose owners are unknown. The entire list should be confined to page 1 in your notebook, front and back if necessary.

Many towns also have separate computerized and alphabetized lists of their property taxpayers. These tax rolls may include owner-unknown entities. This compilation (usually referred to by the assessor's office as the "Owner" or "Alpha" Index), where available, is the best short-cut I know for untitled lot discovery. Some municipalities are more subtle and list owner-unknown parcels by omission. An example of this would be, say, a listing of lots on map 5 that showed 20 parcels but referenced only 19, lot 9 having no ownership designation. If you do encounter a situation like this, do not assume that the parcel with the omitted reference is indeed owner-unknown; the omission may just be an error. Check with the assessor as to the status of the lot. Occasionally you may come across the word "Dropped." This means that the land in question has been joined with another parcel, usually one that is adjacent. Checking the map section will verify this, if you see a connecting bar between the two properties.

The selection of a locus will depend on a number of factors, including your particular interest, how motivated and ambitious you are, how wide you are willing to cast your net, and how much time and money you are willing to invest. Ideally, each owner-unknown project, at completion, should bring you money and/or assets, fulfillment, and satisfaction. But some will entail more or less effort and aggravation than others and, as a tradeoff, promise bigger or more modest payoffs. Hence it is important to know, before choosing a locus, what your priorities and objectives, as well as your capabilities, are. Large parcels of land, often historical in nature, pose more problems but stand to be more rewarding both emotionally and financially. Because they involve more work and produce much frustration, your commitment in these cases must be absolute. By contrast, owner-unknown lots within an established subdivision present fewer difficulties but are generally less rewarding. Although much of the legwork may already have been done for you, most of the benefits to be reaped in that geographical vicinity may already have been harvested.

If you do choose a modest parcel to test the waters, make sure that the lot isn't too small. By this I mean avoid lots that are unbuildable because of size, shape, or the inherent impossibility of conforming to setback and/or road frontage requirements. Local regulations regarding construction permits will be found at the office of the building inspector or the planning board of the municipality in question. Most of these small, often irregular parcels are the residue of old subdivisions. They remain unclaimed precisely because of their perceived worthlessness. These "gores," as they are commonly called, may have value only to an abutter, and may not return an adequate reimbursement for time spent.

Besides size, location is another consideration when choosing a locus. Landlocked lots may seem least desirable because of their presumed lack of access. In fact, these pieces are rarely inaccessible. There may be access rights granted in past deeds, by state statute, or by a planning document. Plans may call for access by a way that has not been constructed yet, a "paper road," as it is known. You can put in this road yourself, which will obviously raise the cost of the project. One suggestion to defray the cost of a road is to ask abutters and others whose property will benefit from greater accessibility to share expenses. There may be instances where the inaccessibility may result from one or more abutters having encroached upon a parcel of land, and so invaded its right of way. Thus, parcels that appear to be inaccessible do have value and offer opportunities that are at least worth checking out.

Owner-unknown lots with water frontage, if there are any such prizes still around, are the most desirable and are the easiest to sell. Before doing any work on these properties, however, make sure they are not swamp land. If you decide to tackle a buildable waterfront lot that is not wetland and is truly owner-unknown, be prepared for the adventure of your life. This type of parcel is, potentially, very valuable but may be extremely difficult to resolve. In most cases, someone, usually a local, has tried unsuccessfully to clear the title. In no way does this mean that the parcel is unobtainable, only that some previous party tried and failed. Don't be detoured by someone else's failures.

Indeed, failure—whether another's or one's own—can motivate you like nothing else. People may still be working on this project, so proceed with caution and tight lips. As with all projects, big or small, be creative and confident. Remember: the greater the challenge, the richer the fulfillment.

The choice is now yours. In your notebook, assign two full pages to each owner-unknown parcel you intend to research. The first page, front and back, will be for all your notes on that specific parcel. The second page is for flowcharts and consolidation and reorganization of your work. Be sure to refer to the lot by the town assessor's number, which, again, usually consists of a map and a parcel number. A sample locus might be referred to as map 8, parcel 16. Locate this parcel in the maps section of the assessor's book, being sure to photocopy the map. Write all pertinent information at the top of the copy and highlight your locus with a yellow fluorescent marker. (I have found it useful to staple the assessor's map to the back of the research sheet.) Before leaving the maps section, note the street and nearest crossroad and make a list of the abutters' map and parcel numbers. Then turn back to the parcel-to-owner cross reference, find the names of your abutters, and write them on both your research sheet and the copy of the assessor's map. The last section of the assessor's book, "owner information," contains the owners' addresses and may also include parcel size and the date of the last transaction involving the property. Use it to learn as much as you can about your abutters. This information is important, as the deed of an abutter may give clues to the identity of a previous owner of your locus.

Bear in mind that the assessor's number may not be the only reference number for a parcel of land. Where land has been developed, subdivision lot numbers are assigned by the planner, surveyor, or engineer, and these have no correlation to the assessor's numbering system. Subdivision numbers were used in many of the old tax records because whereas the assessor's numbers changed from year to year as parcels were combined and divided, the developer's numbers remained constant.

The translation from assessor's map and parcel number to subdivision lot number is necessary only in the case of subdivided land and is relatively simple. A trip down the hall to the building inspector's office should tell you the name of the subdivision. Usually there are maps on the wall for reference, but if you don't find what you are looking for, ask someone. Asking for directions to an area near your locus and following up with a question pertaining to the name of that section in town will yield the answers you seek without broadcasting your intentions. Although you will want to keep the project confidential until you hold title to the land, you may have to risk some exposure in order to obtain information. If you are well received, you might want to follow up further with some specifics, such as asking when the section was subdivided. If you are unable to cross-reference the assessor's map and the subdivision plans through your inquiry, you will need to obtain a copy of the plans at the Registry of Deeds (more on this later) and correlate the numbers that way before you proceed. In any case, the translation *must* be done. Our sample locus, map 8, parcel 16, turns out to be lot 5 in Pinewood Place subdivision, north section, Farmington, Massachusetts.

The last stop in the town hall (and another "must" if your focus is subdivided land) is the vault. Most towns have a safe room for storage of old documents, including maps, vital statistics, and tax records. You can generally gain entrance by talking to the tax collector, the town clerk, or the town assessor. Again, try not to volunteer too much information. If you know when the area was subdivided, ask to see a tax book from approximately five years later, as most of the lots should have been sold by then. Old tax books are wonderful sources of both pertinent and peripheral data. They list owners' names, taxes paid, and sometimes acreages, locations, sections, lot numbers, owner addresses, occupations, and even the names of persons from whom the parcels were purchased. Since at this point in the project you have only the assessor's numbers and (hopefully) the subdivision lot number, you still have a long way to go, and so you would do well to search each tax book for clues that could facilitate the task ahead. Ask for tax books for specific years, say, 1890, 1910, and 1930. It is useful to remember that many parcels of land were lost during wartime and after the stock market crash of 1929. I have resorted to tax books and employed this technique fairly often, and though the process can be quite tedious, I have always found it rewarding. Concentrate especially on the land description column and jot down relevant items in your notebook.

In using this approach, assign a full page at the back of your notebook, where it will be easily accessible, and title it "Tax Records," including for each entry the year, township name, and any changes of ownership. Look for patterns to develop. While paging through the tax records over the forty years between 1890 and 1930 you might discover land in your section repeatedly emanating from one person or group of persons. Chances are that person was the proprietor of the entire section and subdivided the parcel as it appears today. You may also uncover a certain period during which there was no activity, or a time when there was considerable activity—either of which is significant. For example, in the 1890 tax book there is no mention of Forest Hills, yet in 1910 one hundred lots changed hands in this subdivision. Given this set of facts, you may choose to examine other tax books, such as the 1900 volume, for further clarification. Gradually you will be able to narrow the time frame for the first conveyance of your specific lot and its grantor.

Having gathered the basic materials and information at the town hall, you are now in a position to continue the paper search at the Registry of Deeds. Normally located at the county seat, this is the main local municipal authority that houses public land records, though it bears mentioning that some states, such as Connecticut, record and store their land conveyances in the town hall. We will discuss the Registry of Deeds shortly. *The Source* (published by Ancestry Publishing Company, Salt Lake City, Utah), as well as other references found in Appendix 9, will lead you to more specific and esoteric repositories of land records that may be required in certain special situations.

Site Inspection

A t this point you may be anxious to rush over to the Registry of Deeds, but permit me another word of wisdom: first you should visit the site. If you arrive at the locus and there is evidence of recent building or occupation, as far as I'm concerned you've reached a dead end. Abandon this particular project. As a matter of principle, I am opposed to interfering with or undermining anyone's homesite; nor do I condone the use of the methods described in this book to any such end. Furthermore, such a parcel may already have been claimed by adverse possession. I would, however, notify the town assessor as to my findings so that the ownership becomes officially recorded and the owner pays his fair share of taxes.

Should you arrive at the parcel in question and it appears to be raw land, search for landmarks. Such landmarks may include boundary markers, paths, wells, and/or bodies of water. These may be helpful references when determining whether a deed you find is indeed for your locus. Be as precise as possible in regard to these landmarks. For example, if you encounter boundary markers, measure the distance between them and note the types of markers. The kinds of markers most frequently encountered are granite bounds, concrete bounds, metal poles, a stake and stones, a pile of stones, a stake in a tree, or holes. Four granite bounds might indicate that this land was originally staked out but not recently surveyed. You may find two concrete bounds and two stake-in-stones bounds, which may indicate that this land has never been surveyed and that the boundaries were established by the abutters collectively. This point is important to bear in mind

11

during your deed search because the abutters may have encroached upon your land and therefore the deed description will not square with your on-site evaluation.

Finding a boundary is not always easy. In fact, it gets harder from winter to spring and from year to year. Many of these markers have been driven so far into the ground that just the tops remain above the surface. These bounds can easily be obscured by overgrowth and fallen leaves, so look carefully. I remember spending days in the field with three friends and a surveyor looking for one bound—and we knew where it was! Conversely, there are times when you will find two bounds, say five feet apart, and you just know that isn't the way it should be. That's real estate. Such annoyances come with the territory, so to speak. Just take note of the problem. Maybe the finding will provide a clue to ownership, or maybe you've stumbled on the glitch that caused the land to be labeled "owner unknown." In either case, flag the bounds with fluorescent orange surveyor's tape for easy rediscovery.

Now it's time to stroll around the grounds and really get to know this piece of land. Take your notebook along as you canvass the site and record anything of interest. Sometimes lost pieces of land house old burial grounds, which may aid you in the search for the last known owner. What you hope not to find are wetlands or wetland vegetation. One or both of these will most likely cause the lot to be unbuildable, which narrows its marketability and hence lowers the value of the locus. The laws protecting wetlands will vary from state to state. These laws exist for your protection as a potential builder as well as to protect fragile ecosystems. For the specifics in your area, contact the local conservation commission. You may also spot or learn of a municipal dump nearby, another circumstance that will diminish the value of the property. Many supposed owner-unknown lots are found near these refuse areas. These parcels were abandoned because of their perceived worthlessness. However, don't dismiss such a lot out of hand, as the land may be valuable to the town and, once having claimed it, you can sell it for cash or other valuable consideration, or make a gift of it, which can be deducted from your income taxes in most cases. And the purchase of such a parcel is usually much easier to negotiate with an heir or heirs.

On your way out of an overgrown parcel you may notice trash or papers. Clean up the area. It's good for the environment, it's a good excuse to be on the land, and you may even find a clue sending you hightailing to the Registry of Deeds. Stranger things have happened.

Registry of Deeds

The Registry of Deeds is both a mine and a minefield. Filled with illuminating answers, undetected mistakes, and apparent contradictions with regard to historical real estate transactions, it must be approached with both curiosity and care. This longstanding government institution is usually located at the county courthouse and is dedicated to property recordkeeping and the communication of information relating to those records. When entering a registry of deeds, take a quick look around the various rooms and then have one of the clerks explain the nature and organization of the registry's data. Each registry is arranged differently and may house records of more or less value and interest. Frequently consulted indexes and catalogs are usually kept in the research or examination room. Additional rooms common to most registries of deeds are the registrar's office and the vault; these may contain damaged, oversized, uncataloged, or superannuated plans and records. Don't be afraid to explore and ask questions. One of the registries I visited was accommodating enough to list properties in its jurisdiction by owner, and even included owner-unknown entries. Another registry housed such treasures as local history books, old records of town meetings and proprietors' records, each of which offered something of value. The town meeting records helped clarify vague areas in crucial deeds, while the proprietors' records lent corroboration and brought to light new facts and names to research.

If you were able to place any owner on your locus through the old tax books, you should proceed first in the Registry of Deeds to the grantor index. Ideally, this index should contain an entry for all real estate transactions, and all real estate transactions in the county should be referenced here. However, conveyances can be referenced in the grantor and grantee indexes only if they have been properly recorded at the Registry of Deeds. There are two sets of these books, one for registered land (where there is clear ownership by land court decree) and another for unregistered land (where there is no land court involvement). Both must be searched. They are generally located in different sections of the registry and refer to particular deed books. The deed books are organized chronologically. You will want to find the book that corresponds to the time period the alleged owner paid taxes.

If, for instance, you found Joe Johnson paying taxes on the locus referenced as lot 5, Pinewood Place, in 1905, you would get the grantor book dated 1896-1906. As mentioned before, each registry is different and will use its own cataloging system. If you cannot find what you are looking for, ask someone. This book is the appropriate place to begin your grantor schedule because Joe was paying taxes on the locus and therefore was the owner of record during the period covered in this book. The grantor index, following the present example, would tell you if Joe Johnson sold this land before 1907 and to whom. Continue the search in ascending chronological order until you find the conveyance of this land. You must check all transactions to date emanating from Joe Johnson.

You may find an entry in the grantor index dated 1920-1929. First, copy that page so you have a record of having found and examined this document. Make notes on the copy and refile the book so that others may use it. The entry of this conveyance in the grantor index should contain the date of the transaction, the grantor (seller), the grantee (acquirer), the location, and the book/page where the document can be found.

In this instance, Joe Johnson's conveyance listed the grantee as Ralph Porter. It was dated December 9, 1922, and could be found in book 131, on page 357. The book referred to in this hypothetical case is the book of deeds, Squires County, unregistered land section. I find most of my material in the unregistered land section because the actual ownership of an owner-unknown parcel predates the land court. Also, registered land usually does not become owner-unknown, because the potential for questionable ownership, past or present, has been removed by decree.

Find the unregistered land records and pull book 131 from the shelf. If you have the right book there should be a conveyance on page 357 from Joe Johnson to Ralph Porter. Copy this entire deed and put it in the appropriate section of your notebook. It is hard to resist the urge to pick this deed apart, but don't. Registry time is precious and should be used to acquire the rest of the conveyance and testimonial documents relevant to the owner you are searching. If you manage to copy all the entries for this owner, take a lunch break out of the building. Then you can review these records in privacy and at your leisure.

There are several types of records you will encounter in the unregistered land books. These documents include mortgages, lien releases, powers of attorney, affidavits, and testimonials, as well as quitclaim, warranty, exchange, and confirmatory deeds. (Before you rush to your dictionary, be assured I will define these terms in due course.) All of these documents, if applicable to your locus and owner of record, can effect the project drastically. In the case where Joe Johnson does not convey this locus, but does grant power of attorney to Kevin Tyler, the appointee could sell this land. This transfer may only be found under Kevin Tyler, so you have a new name to research. As spelling was somewhat arbitrary in olden days, get in the habit of searching similar and alternative versions of surnames. It's a good research technique. In the case of the above, one might scan Tyler and Tiler. But perhaps we are getting ahead of ourselves here. Let's back up for a moment and examine the subject of deeds.

Deeds

A deed is a method, or tool, of conveying ownership of property. The registration of deeds is of critical importance, as it provides a public record establishing an opinion of ownership. Over the years there have been many different forms of deeds. The ensuing paragraphs will introduce you to the most common types used in real estate transactions.

The *quitclaim deed* is the most common means of real estate conveyance that I have come across, although its popularity may vary from region to region. Land transfers with quitclaim covenants are conveyances of "all right, title and interest, if any," implying no guarantee of good right to sell or title purity, although assurance phrases can be added to firm up the transaction and protect the buyer. To ascertain the value of these documents, examine the land description and interest passed to the grantor throughout his title chain.

A *warranty deed* is similar to a quitclaim deed, except that it contains an assurance phrase. Typically, it will read as follows: "That the grantor, for himself, his heirs, and assigns, have good right to sell, grant, convey, and release these premises free from all encumbrances, and shall warrant and defend the same to the grantee and his heirs, successors, and assigns forever, against the lawful claims and demands of all persons."

Commissioner's deeds are usually granted by decree of the court handling probate affairs. This is an equity matter whereby an interested party petitions the court in an attempt to garner all outstanding interests in a parcel of land. Equity issues are usually interest discrepancies or partition disputes that require court interdiction to determine who gets which piece of land, how big it should be, and what will become of the unrepresented interest. Often this is the remedy of choice to settle family squabbles over inherited real property. The names of all interested parties are advertised for a certain period of time. Once all claims are disposed of to the satisfaction of the commissioner, an auction will take place and the court will adjudicate the proceedings. Monies are placed in escrow for owners that come forth thereafter, and cash distributions are limited to the extent of those funds.

Exchange deeds are relatively self-explanatory. Two named parties describe their respective premises and agree to swap titles. Formerly, neighbors swapped land and then deeded the parcels back to the original owners on the same day. After considerable research into this curious practice, I discovered that this established an official record of the mutually agreed-upon bounds in lieu of costly and time-consuming formal surveys.

Division deeds involve a translation of an adjudicated estate or an agreement between interested parties to partition real property. These deeds serve to clarify terms, confirm boundaries, and specify parcel ownership. When expressing the wishes of a probate or land court, these documents form an important bridge between the Registry of Deeds and the court system. These divisions should be examined carefully, along with all available court files pertinent to the transaction. When you encounter such a deed, it is helpful to sketch the division as in Appendix 5.

There are instances where deeds are flawed—by vague delineation of areas, misrepresentations, or clerical errors—so that the parties may wish to fix them. *Confirmatory deeds* are the best and most common vehicle for correction and clarification of recorded real estate documents. These amended transactions should always make reference to the original conveyance. Both deeds should be scrutinized to ascertain that the changes are correct. The presence of a confirmatory deed in the case of an owner-unknown parcel may offer a clue with respect to the conflict that created the proprietary mystery.

Land court deeds will be found in the registered land section of the Registry of Deeds. This conveyance is similar to the warranty deed in that land and guarantees are given to the grantee. The land court process was created as a curative vehicle for a "cloudy" land title. Each deed is assigned a case file number and is usually accompanied by a certified engineer's or surveyor's plan of the premises. Remember that this form of deed is a decree, not a compilation of the facts. If one of these deeds is associated with your locus, obtain the complete case file from the land court. Call or write the land court to find out how to obtain the information. The phone number and address can usually be found in the telephone directory's blue pages or government listings under "Courts."

Despite the differences between these various deeds, they also contain many common elements. Someone, of somewhere, who got something from someone else, conveys something, somewhere, sometime, and somehow, for some reason, to someone else, of somewhere. As confusing as that statement is, it is the essence of a deed. Let us begin to assign names to these deed elements. The first "someone" is the grantor, of some designated address, who has the right to sell because of a title he holds to a property in a subdivision, town, and state, which he agrees to convey on a specific date, for consideration (usually money), to the grantee of a specified city, county, and state. To be more specific, the example may be phrased thus: "I, Joe Johnson, of the township of Farmington, and in the county of Squires County, State of Massachusetts, owner of lot 5 in Pinewood Place, north section, bought of Matthew Allen, referenced in deed book 101, page 519, in the Squires County Registry of Deeds, and dated March 15, 1898, having good right, grant, give, sell, bargain, and convey for myself, my heirs, successors and assigns, all my right title and interest, in lot 5, found on a plan of land called Pinewood Place, recorded at the Squires County Registry of Deeds and a plan numbered 1119 in Farmington, Massachusetts, on this 9th Day of December, 1922, for the sum of 250.00 dollars paid in hand by Ralph Porter of same township, county and state, for himself, his heirs and assigns, forever." This statement should be followed by a more descriptive land clause, though not necessarily, since most of the relevant information can be found on the plan referred to in the deed. As a final common element, a witnessed or notarized signature and a recording date with acceptance signature from the registrar will be found at the bottom of the deed.

There are, then, certain standard elements that must be contained in a document to validate a real estate transaction in most states. Understanding a deed, and its format, is vital before you can proceed with confidence. Pay close attention to the wording used in the deeds you research. This knowledge will give you valuable insight in the preparation of conveyance tools you will have to use yourself to consolidate the claim on your owner-unknown locus. I personally feel that deed examination is best accomplished at home, or in some other private and controlled environment. So go home, take a break, and then dig in.

Homework

Find your favorite chair, adjust the reading light, gather your writing implements, and retrieve the notes you copied at the Registry of Deeds. Lighting is a small but crucial matter. When studying deeds, always examine documents under the best lighting conditions. I cannot emphasize this enough, as inadequate light contributes to eye strain, erroneous interpretation, drowsiness, and overall inefficiency. Some of the documents that you will encounter may be very old and extremely hard to read. They may be faded, tattered, and scrawled. Do not hesitate to use a magnifying glass if the need arises. I find it most helpful to accent key information with a fluorescent, wide-tip "highlighter." (Among the various brands, I recommend Major Accent fluorescent yellow markers, which seem to cause the highlighted areas to jump out at you, even with the poorest-quality records.) Accent the grantor(s), grantee(s), parcel description(s), title references, town location, subdivision, transaction date, and recording date. After noting the grantor, I focus on the town and subdivision locations. If my locus is in Farmington, and the deed refers to land in Medview, the document is not considered locus. You must make sure, however, that the document contains no additional conveyance phrase such as "and all my land in Squires County" that could constitute a transfer of said locus.

You may be unsure of the relevance of a deed. My rule is: If it's questionable, possible, or close, copy it. You may waste a few dollars and a little time, but this painstaking practice usually pays off in the end. There have been documents I initially passed over because, at the time, they meant nothing to me; then, as I became further involved in the project, I looked at them in a different light and realized their significance. So copy everything. File these potentially relevant papers in a folder labeled "Miscellaneous" and leaf through them from time to time.

In the event that you find a straight conveyance of the locus, read the complete deed carefully to ascertain the acreage, percentage sold, and any other tidbits that may come into play, such as divisions, sections, landmarks, and past owners or partner allocations. Turning to the actual parcel description, take the time to absorb every detail. On the corner of the deed, begin to sketch the orientation and dimensions of the land, noting all abutter references. Check the references while re-reading the deed, and, if correct, reproduce and enlarge this sketch on the back of the deed with precision and clarity. The land description may give you dimensions and the types of bounds used in marking the parcel. Compare this information with the notes on your visit to the site. If the data is consistent with the notes, you're in good shape. If there is a discrepancy, then maybe this deed is not locus, or the parcel was modified by a later conveyance. This may tip you off to a division of the land that you may find in the registry. In most jurisdictions, engineer's plans must be approved by the planning board, then recorded at the registry, before land can be subdivided. The deed itself may refer to a specific plan name and number. The registry clerks can tell you how to obtain a copy of this plan, or plat, as it is commonly referred to, for your records. Highlight the rest of the records like the above deed, making reference notes in the margin of the grantor index copies. Marginal comments should include specific location, transaction date, statement of "locus" or "not locus," name of significant abutter, specified encumbrances such as rights of way, interest passed, and the type of instrument.

There are times during a title examination when you may come across two or more conveyances of the same property by different parties. Most often this occurs when interests are held and conveyed separately by *tenants in common,* a form of cooperative ownership often created when land passes by decree to the heirs-at-law from the decedent's adjudicated estate. In the case of owner-unknown land, one must garner all the divided interests, through deeds or decree, to hold clear title. *Joint tenancy* is another form of multiple ownership. However, in this case of non-inventoried land, a category that applies to most owner-unknown parcels, the land passes by right of survivorship, unless otherwise stipulated. So, let's take the example of three persons who receive (or are "devised") real property, in joint tenancy, by the death of a grandfather who died intestate. The last one alive owns the land "absolutely." From there the land would pass, by state statute, to the heirs of the last owner, though there are special situations when this is not so. Leave those intricacies to the hired experts, the lawyers and their title examiners.

The other common situation that causes multiple conveyances of a particular piece of land is a *dual title chain*. This turns up in areas where, for example, the native Indians deeded land, and the governing sovereign deeded out the same land, but to a different party. In fact, this is the problem underlying many owner-unknown parcels. Land was so inexpensive and plentiful on the frontier in previous centuries that it wasn't worth fighting for, especially when there was no structure involved like a house or barn, and so competing claims would go unresolved.

There is one other conveyance oddity that bears explanation. In the course of your title search you may come across the deeding out of a certain tract of land only to notice that same land being deeded back to the original owner on the same day. Apparently, at one time this was an inexpensive yet legally binding way to settle a boundary dispute between neighbors without involving courts, lawyers, and/or surveyors.

After poring over the mound of paperwork you generated at the registry, one of two conclusions should be evident: either the latest grantee sold the property, or he didn't. If he did convey the locus, you have a new grantor schedule to run. If he did not convey this land, then double check the grantor books for missed entries and re-evaluate the deeds you copied. If, at this point, you are reasonably sure that there was no conveyance of the locus, your next stop is the Registry of Probate.

The quiet of night is a good time to take inventory. Sit at a large desk and lay out all relevant documents, including maps, notes, and deeds. This will allow you to integrate your information. Do the deeds correspond with the maps and the on-site inspection notes? If not, why, and what are the inconsistencies? Bear in mind that most title transactions are logical when viewed with the benefit of hindsight. It is important to focus on any questionable items and to resolve them, because if a deed does not make sense to you, it won't make sense to a potential buyer or his lawyer. Finding answers to your questions systematically, step by step, should be your short-term goal. The process will sustain your enthusiasm and keep you on track. At this point your assessment plan might sound something like this: "I have a locus, I discovered a previous owner (Joe Johnson), and I found a conveyance of the locus to Ralph Porter in December of 1922. I must run a grantor schedule for Ralph Porter (1922 to date), get a copy of Farmington subdivision plan 1119, and copy Joe Johnson's title reference deed from Matthew Allen, located in book 101, page 519."

States usually have title standards that require only a sixty-year search. These standards have been adopted to facilitate the transfer of title by limiting the transaction period that must be researched, and thus the number of possible encumbrances on the locus. In my opinion, these standards undermine both law and history. The practice is unfortunate because it permits superficial research to establish title. That title may then be used to establish other claims based on the same half-truth. By the time the appropriate history is exhumed, presumption, and perhaps error or injustice, has dominoed over the land. This may cause great incongruities in adjacent titles. If an abutter title chain is derived in this manner, it will be of limited value in the owner-unknown discovery phase because most parcels of owner-unknown land have been so labeled for more than sixty years, and some for more than 100 years. It is also quite possible that this abutter has encroached on your land. To do these projects properly, you must respect history. And in honoring history, you have the satisfaction of knowing you have acted nobly. You may even clarify or correct certain aspects of local folklore, rewriting them in the process. Such are the intangible rewards I spoke of that will bring extra enjoyment to your efforts.

The last item that needs attention here is the flowchart. This is a concise graph demonstrating land passage. As presented in Appendix 6, the flowchart displays, in descending chronological order, periods of both activity and inactivity, providing your assessment plan with visual direction from beginning to end. At this stage of our sample project there are two points of "recess," or temporary stopping points. One point is Ralph Porter, who needs to be researched in the grantor books to the time when he conveys the locus, or up to the present date, showing no conveyance of locus. The other point of recess is Matthew Allen. Most flowcharts use arrows to display the direction of land transfer. The date of transaction should appear on one side of the arrow, with book and page reference on the other. When you are done with a project, the title chain should flow from the first recorded conveyance, through all subsequent transactions, and terminate with present (living) owners, be they direct grantees or heirs.

Now, take a few deep breaths and let the project go for the night.

Back to the County Courthouse

I t's not unusual to wake up from a night's sleep with new questions and ideas to add to the assessment plan. Your subconscious has surely been working on the project. Title examiners talk about "living with a title." This project can be the second spouse, or lover, you take to bed at night.

Gather your title-examining tools, your notebook, and your flow-chart, and hasten back to the Registry of Deeds. You may wish to purchase a briefcase on the way and stuff all your goodies inside for safe-keeping. As you pull up to the courthouse for a second time, it should dawn on you that this is an awfully large building to house just the county registries. Indeed there are many other records there, and much of the complex is a relatively untapped resource. Most county court-houses contain legal reference material, files of rejected and pending land court cases, blank forms needed in various court proceedings, and archives of general court records. On a recent trip to one such institution I was given a countywide directory that contained a grid map of the cities and towns within its jurisdiction and provided useful infor-mation, including pertinent phone numbers and addresses, in a concise, convenient format. The directory also furnished historical information and dates of special events, both local and regional. Make a point of asking the county clerk or a receptionist if they have such a directory or fact sheet.

The first assignment on today's agenda is to find plan 1119 in Farm-ington. As always, obtain a copy of the plan and study it at home. These plans are quite large and must be copied by a special ammonia

27

process. You can request a copy from the registrar or contact the engineering firm that prepared the subdivision plan. Subdivisions are recorded segmentations of land, layed out in accordance with local planning and zoning regulations. If a proprietor wishes to subdivide a parcel, he must engage an engineer and a surveyor to prepare such a plan. In brief, the surveyor is responsible for the segmentation of the entire parcel and the specifics of the lots created by said division; the engineer handles the road layouts, pier planning, sewage, and drainage. The county registrar will record only plans that have been prepared and certified by appropriately accredited and licensed professionals.

Take note of the name and date of the plan for reference. Look carefully at the plan and see if it coincides with what you have seen in the field and read in the deeds. In pencil, lightly make notes on the map of any discrepancies. If indeed your locus is in this subdivision, highlight the parcel. Label the abutters, indicating the owners of record and any names that appear on these adjacent parcels in your deed research. Open your notebook to the flowchart and write the name of the person(s) who caused this plan to be created. For our purposes, the plan reference number 1119 in Farmington, Squires County, refers to a layout of Pinewood Place, dated February 7, 1892, prepared for Silas Smith, by William Tappan. Silas Smith is known as the developer of this subdivision. Your title chain should go back at least to this owner, as he was the original proprietor of the whole parcel before subdivision. A gap in the flowchart has been created between Silas Smith and Matthew Allen. To answer the questions posed by this void you can run a grantor schedule on Silas Smith or a grantee schedule on Matthew Allen. Either of these should achieve the same result.

The grantee indexes are similar to the grantor indexes in mechanics and organization, with the exception that title flows in the opposite direction. The grantee index is designed to trace the roots of real property. Referring back to our example, you might look up Matthew Allen as a grantee and find a conveyance to him from Silas Smith. This entry is dated October 5, 1896 and can be found in book 99, on page 17, and is labeled in the margin as lots 1-30 inclusive, in Pinewood Place, north section. Copy it.

For those of you who have not found a previous taxpayer for the selected locus, the grantee index can also be used as an alternative method of owner discovery. By running grantee schedules on the abutters, eventually you should find some reference to a previous owner. The abutter information should have been obtained from the assessor's book and copied onto project page 1 in your notebook. You may also have noted year or book and page references to the abutters' conveyances. Any of this information will save tedious research time. To continue the sample case, the abutters, stated respectively, north, south, east, and west, are Charles Folger, Rufus Tabor, "owner unknown," and Cedar Street. Charles Folger's deed is referenced in the assessor's book by the date 1923. Gather the grantee index for that year and locate the entry for Charles Folger. A transaction is found under grantee Charles E. Folger, dated December 12, 1922, and with Ralph Porter listed as the grantor. The book and page reference is 131/359. Does that sound familiar?

Over the years, especially with older deeds, I have noticed that conveyances within certain sections of town were recorded nearly simultaneously and may be found one after the other in the index. This has been attributed to the hardships associated with travelling to the county seat. To cut down on these trips, families and neighbors compiled records and registered them in one sitting. In theory, this was a good idea; however, these papers were subject to loss and destruction. This gathering and holding of unrecorded documents is one of the common explanations in broken title chains and one of the ways land acquires owner-unknown status. I have made a practice of paging through previous and subsequent deeds whenever I access the unregistered land records. This can save you time, add perspective, and even reveal records that were erroneously cataloged or omitted altogether. The grantor and grantee indexes exist as a system of checks and balances; therefore each deed should be referenced in both books.

The conveyance by deed, dated December 12, 1922, should appear in the grantee index under Charles Folger and in the grantor index under Ralph Porter. As you will see below, this is not the case. The lesson here is not to presume that a document does not exist just because you have not found it. If you don't find this particular deed in the grantor book, check the grantee index. You may have to go through the alternate route to discover both grantor and grantee. To help put this example in perspective, look at your plan. When two different names appear on the same premises, one in one year and another in a later year, there should be a paper trail between the two, the name appearing earlier being the grantor and the later-referenced owner being the grantee. This may occur directly via a single entry or by a series of transactions.

Last, run a grantor schedule on Ralph Porter. As you page through the grantor index you see no entries for Ralph Porter, but as you recheck your work, you notice an entry in 1926 for a Ralph Potter. You find this deed and notice that the grantor's name is indeed Ralph Porter, but had been typed or spelled incorrectly in the index. Clerical mistakes like this can cause enough confusion to create an illusion of non-conveyance or owner-unknown land. The tax bill on the property may have been undeliverable in Potter's name, thus leading to an owner-unknown conclusion. After a cursory reading through this deed you determine that it is not locus because the conveyance has to do with land in the neighboring township of Byron. Let us now assume that you check all the grantor indexes and find no conveyance of this land. Note that the conveyance from Porter to Folger in 1922 was omitted from the grantor records. For the record, that deed conveyed the abutting property only, and is considered not locus. The conclusion drawn from all available data is that Ralph Porter is the last known owner of lot 5, at Pinewood Place, in Farmington, Massachusetts. As a safety measure, complete schedules should be run on him, documenting everything coming to Ralph and everything conveyed by him. This method of checks and balances supports our conjecture that Ralph Porter is, indeed, the registry's last known owner. To find out what became of him and the land, you must check the Registry of Probate.

Registry of Probate

The Registry of Probate is the recordkeeping body of Probate Court, also know as Family Court. This court has jurisdiction over such matters as divorces, name changes, guardianships, some equity matters, and estate proceedings. The actual name of the court may vary from state to state. In New York, for instance, probate matters are handled in the Surrogate's Court. In other states probate courts are designated as Ordinary Court and Orphan's Court. There are two primary types of probate files that deal with land of a deceased "last known owner." Those who leave a will are said to have died testate, and those whose estates are at the mercy of the probate court are said to have died intestate. The procedures are quite different for each situation, so you must determine which status applies in the case of your project.

When a will is submitted to the probate court for acceptance, there are many legal and bureaucratic steps that must be transacted. The presenter is appointed by the decedent and is called the *executor* of the estate in question. Usually a lawyer or a relative (or both) is selected to carry out the will of the decedent; whichever the case, the party must be recognized by the court. The executor is responsible for the accounting and supervision of the estate, including paying outstanding bills, posting a bond, making funeral arrangements, taking inventory of real and personal property, ordering appraisals, providing a list containing next of kin and heirs, accounting of debit/asset ratio, managing trusts, facilitating decedent bequests, distributing assets, and reporting to the court. To settle the estate, these tasks must be completed, documented, then accepted by court decree. All relevant documents are compiled and cataloged for reference in what is known as a probate docket. In our hypothetical case, you would be looking for either the probate file of Ralph Porter containing his last wishes, or a court-assigned account and dispensation of his worldly possessions. The docket number is I-811, Squires County. Make a copy of this entire file for your records. As these are complicated proceedings, you may need to review the file several times to become sufficiently familiar with it.

We find that our last known owner, Ralph Porter, died intestate, January 7, 1948. Since he left no will and designated no executor, the probate court judge would most likely have appointed an attorney to settle his estate. This *administrator* must employ the state statutes governing intestacy, in this instance contained in the *Massachusetts General Laws,* to determine the passage of his property.

Whether the decedent in question died testate or intestate, an inventory must be filed. This listing is generally found in two separate schedules: one for personal property and another for real property. Very often land becomes owner-unknown because it does not appear in the probated inventory. The administrator or executor can only cite land or interest if they know of its existence. In cases where the last known owner dies intestate, any forgotten item passes in the same manner as the itemized listings. There is, however, a curative phrase used in will preparation that deals with items omitted from the inventory. The "rest, residue, and remainder" clause allows the specified grantee to inherit everything the decedent is found to own, even if not itemized in the probate inventory. Inventoried land may also become lost if the deed description is too vague, the interest is negligible, there are extensive taxes due, the land is perceived to be worthless, or any combination of the above.

The schedule of beneficiaries found in the probate file warrants close analysis. This roster should contain the names and locations of all heirs and next of kin. The spouse and/or blood relatives become the sole heirs to an estate, by statute, when the decedent dies intestate, or, in testate cases, by default, when there is no rest, residue, and remainder clause in the will and the locus does not appear in the inventory. Under certain circumstances, adopted children share in the estate as natural offspring. In Ralph Porter's case, he left three children: sons Peter, whereabouts unknown, and Samuel, unmarried, and a married daughter, Victoria Tyler, wife of attorney Kevin Tyler. These three, Peter, Samuel, and Victoria, each hold a one-third interest in the owner-unknown locus. According to the schedule of beneficiaries, Samuel lives in the township of Byron, in Squires County, and Victoria lives nearby in Summerset, Queens County. Information gleaned from probate dockets may require additional research in other county court-houses, as turns out to be the case in the above scenario. The Genealogical Publishing Company (Baltimore, MD) has an extraor-dinary reference guide to probate repositories called *County Court-house Book*, by Elizabeth Bentley. Buy it. The book will pay for itself.

Usually you will find a probate docket only in the county or town where the decedent actually died, and only if an estate went through the court system. Each state has its own statutes regarding probatable assets and the necessity of filing when survived by a spouse. This infor-mation should be learned before proceeding. Legislation concerning real property can be found in the state general laws, which are usually available at the law library within the courthouse. The same informa-tion can be gained from handbooks or, for a fee, from title examiners or conveyance lawyers.

While you are in the probate office you can check for files under the names of Peter Porter, Samuel Porter, and Victoria Tyler. You will have to go to the historical society to locate the missing Peter Porter, and to Queens County for Victoria's probate, but before you leave the courthouse go back to the Registry of Deeds and run these three heirs as grantors. It is unlikely that they would have conveyed the locus but, for the sake of completeness, you must make sure.

There may also be information regarding these heirs in other trans-actions, alerting you, possibly, to changes in name or venue. Let's say you find the search unremarkable, so you proceed to the Queens County Registry of Probate. There you find probate files for both Samuel and Victoria. Samuel dies March 18, 1973, testate, probate number DI-9854, leaving his sister, Victoria Tyler, as administratrix and sole beneficiary. Victoria dies April 25, 1978, probate number DI-9934, survived only by her spouse, Kevin Tyler, who realizes her entire estate. This information should now be organized in a concise and correlative manner.

To keep all this information under control, and to show at a glance the descent of hereditary interest in the land from one generation to the next, I recommend constructing a "descendancy chart" (see Appendix 7). The chart begins by placing the last known owner, in this case Ralph Porter, in generation 1 at the left side of the form. His spouse also appears in generation 1, directly below him, or, if more than one spouse, directly above him. His children are placed in generation 2, their children in generation 3, and thus the chart continues until living heirs are reached. Each box in the chart should contain sufficient room to allow you to list pertinent facts about the individual—birthdate (B), marriage date (M), date of death (D), location of probate file (Pb#), and spouse information. This will come in handy, as it reveals the gaps in your research and is a reminder to you of work that needs to be done. (A reversal of this chart, an ancestry chart, or pedigree, is useful in showing how the last known owner inherited the land in question.)

Our latest information, then, is that the locus we have been examining is owned by two people, Peter Porter and Kevin Tyler, with a one-third and two-thirds interest, respectively. To recap the derivation of descended interests from Ralph Porter to Kevin Tyler, let's summarize the pertinent facts. Kevin Tyler's wife, Victoria, obtains a one-third interest from the probate of her decedent father, Ralph Porter, and a one-third interest from her brother Samuel, at his death, by will. At Victoria's death, her entire estate is willed to her husband, Kevin Tyler, including the two-thirds interest in the locus. No probate is found at either registry under Kevin Tyler, and there is no record of any conveyance of this land having been enacted by any instrument. A quick glance at a local phonebook shows Tyler's address and phone number. A call verifies that he is indeed alive. Now you have a living heir with a two-thirds interest in the locus, an individual who can convey that interest to you. The remaining interest is still in Peter Porter, about whom we still have little information. The local historical society is a reasonable next destination for continuing our research, because where there is a residence, as in the case of Ralph Porter, Peter's father, there are usually references.

Historical Societies

H istorical societies are institutions dedicated to keeping our past preserved, organized, and available. Since they are usually privately funded and operated, they often offer weekend and evening hours and thus easy accessibility for the average working person, though they may charge a small admission fee. I used to spend my lunch hours at the registries and town halls and Saturdays at the historical society. Call your local society for hours and fees. Incidentally, it is advantageous to support these institutions by becoming a member. The dues are relatively inexpensive and pay handsomely. The curator and librarian can be very helpful. They can shave hours, if not days, off your quest, as they know just where everything is. For instance, you may not find anything under Matthew Allen, but the librarian, having run across him before, knows that his papers are filed under his legal first name, Jonathan.

Historical society holdings seem to fall into four broad groupings: cataloged items; memorabilia that are shelved but not cataloged; items, usually in the backroom or basement, that have yet to be cataloged; and items which are available elsewhere. Owner-unknown researchers may take advantage of many unique opportunities here. The curator of the local historical society may know of a rare document germane to your locus that was bought by the state historical society. Furthermore, the staff can keep your project in mind when indexing newly arrived material. Historical society archives contain a treasure trove of unrecorded deeds, state censuses, private letters, and maps. Rare historical publications and scores of genealogical records may enable you to trace family histories heretofore obscure or enigmatic.

In the case of the project at hand, you will want to examine any entries under Ralph Porter in the local historical society catalog. You may find references to deeds, maps, personal correspondence, and genealogical compilations. There is a letter indexed under Ralph Porter from Peter Porter. This letter shows Peter's address as 287 Valley Lane, Kent, Rhode Island, and is dated July 4, 1946. By reading on, you discover that Peter was Ralph's son by his first marriage, he was born and raised in the township of Odessa, he was 36 years old at the time of the letter, he has a wife named Sarah, his children are named Melissa and Allison, and he had just returned from World War II. The letter ends with a stirring set of remarks about military missions of platoon 7007 and Peter's role as sergeant.

The historical society's reference catalog will index information vital to your quest in a multitude of ways. In the interest of thoroughness, check the catalog for entries under both the abutter and subdivision names. Referencing the locus, you may uncover plans that label the owner or abutters. You may also wish to search the society's holdings in publications and newspapers for genealogical and historical references. Many historical societies have unpublished compilations of genealogical and cemetery data. These are wonderful sources for both original and corroborative information. If you look up the town as a reference, you may find old town meeting records. These comprehensive, unpublished memoirs may include mention of the subdivision that contains your owner-unknown locus and the parcel's owner(s) and/or abutters. Should you not find living heirs at the local society, you may wish to visit other historical societies, certainly the one in or near the residence of the heir(s) being searched, and possibly your state society and appropriate specialized historical societies.

Census and other vital records are most commonly found in federal and state archives, government and specialized libraries, and other official bureaus, but it is far more convenient to try the local historical society first. In fact, it is not uncommon to find at the local society original census records and bound reprints of birth, marriage, and death records for many other cities and towns in that particular state. Though these are excellent sources of general information, and useful for locating data on family history for earlier periods, these types of records are of limited value for heir searches in the twentieth century, since to ensure the right of privacy most census records are sealed and closed to the public for seventy-two years. (The most recent federal census open to researchers is the one taken in 1910.) However, most states do have access provisions to more recent records for close family members.

With all this information you should be able to track Peter Porter using the methods already described and others soon to be presented. The collected data should help you fill in the ancestral tree. However, it is wise to treat all unofficial and unsubstantiated findings skeptically until you have acceptable documentation to verify their authenticity. For purposes of verification, as you proceed, obtain notarized copies of vital records that contain maternal and paternal references.

In the case of Peter, beginning back at square one, consult a detailed map of Rhode Island. Use the grid reference and township listing, if provided, for the location of Kent and Odessa. You should find Peter's birth certificate in the Odessa town clerk's office or, failing that, at the bureau of vital statistics at the county or state level. Search the years around 1910 because the letter stated that his age was 36 in 1946. This certificate is very important because it identifies Ralph Porter as Peter's father. This is the kind of irrefutable proof required by convey-ance attorneys, insurance underwriters, and title examiners to demon-strate family relationship. There are many Peter Porters, but the birth record designates this particular one as the Peter Porter who is a blood heir, heir-at-law, and rightful descendant of Ralph Porter and his estate. The Coventry County Historical Society has scattered mate-rials relating to Peter and his family, but most of the references concern his enlistment and career in the military. The available documents cover a limited time span and then they just stop. This record pattern, as you will learn with experience, usually denotes a permanent change of family residence.

And so we arrive at yet another detour. Specialized historical and lineage societies as well as other resource facilities, some dealing with black Americans, may offer clues at this point, but a safer bet is to tap next into the vast holdings of the public and private library networking system. See Appendix 10 for a listing of selected reference libraries, including some specialized repositories, organized by state. Checking these auxiliary repositories should be done after exhausting all viable local sources of information, such as the hometown library.

Local Research for Living Heirs

Given the present data, the questions that should follow are: Is Peter Porter alive? If so, where? If not, where did he die, and what became of his wife and children? The search is narrowing, but these remaining concerns are defying easy resolution. After thoroughly scrutinizing the hometown historical society records, visit the local libraries, past known addresses, cemeteries, medical record facilities, and county registries; speak to residents, and go back to the town hall to research the new material you have uncovered.

At the end of these rounds you may finally see the light at the end of the tunnel. The Odessa town vital statistics show a marriage between Sarah Arey of Odessa and Peter Porter, son of Ralph Porter, taking place on December 23, 1935. There are also birth records for Melissa and Allison Porter, twins born to Sarah and Peter Porter at Auburn Hospital on August 25, 1939. All this documentation is necessary in order to authenticate your title chain. However, you are no closer to finding Peter Porter and his family. Coventry's probate and deed registries are devoid of information on Peter and Sarah Porter. This tells you that he didn't own land or die in Coventry County, unless you missed something.

Time for a stop at the local library. The visit could really surprise you. Many of these libraries have a resident genealogist or someone with enough expertise to point you to newspaper clippings, published genealogies, census compilations, and city/town directories. The latter have always been a useful tool for me, as they constitute a concise, reliable, and continuous source of local data. If you have an address and date for the party being researched, as in the case of Peter Porter, you should find him indexed in that year's directory. Ask the librarian for the city/town directory that covers 1946, since the letter we found from Peter Porter to his father Ralph was dated in July of that year. Of the several Peter Porters cited in the 1946 volume, one is listed at 287 Valley Lane in Kent. He is a military officer with two children and a wife named Sarah. At this point you should check the current phonebook for an entry for him. Should there be none, the logical assumption is that he moved sometime between 1946 and the present. An examination of the directories for the intervening years may give you clues to the date of his disappearance. Such inspection shows him at the same location and with the same listing in every book until 1957, when it is noted that he had "removed to Bristol, MA." So, once again, it's back to a Massachusetts probate registry. The county name and seat of any city or town can be obtained by a call to any of several local authorities, including municipal offices or the police department.

The township of Bistol, we discover, is located in Cromwell County, whose courthouse is in Okemos. Exercising the skills already learned, we quickly ascertain that probate D8/526 belongs to Peter Porter. The date of death as reported on the petition reads June 7, 1983. He died a widower and intestate. Listed as the next of kin are two daughters, Melissa McCrumb, wife of Jason McCrumb of Portland, and Allison Porter of Bristol, both in Cromwell County, Massachusetts. There is also a guardianship probate for Allison Porter, with minors Annette and Allan, dated January 31, 1990, and referenced as D9/46. This docket reveals that Allison was incapacitated in an automobile accident and subsequently remanded, along with her minor children, to the custody of her sister Melissa. It is further stated that the father of twins Allan and Annette is unknown, and that mother Allison was never married. For the record, the twins were shaken up but virtually unharmed in the accident.

The issues of legitimacy, incapacity, and minors' inheritance in intestate estates are treated differently from state to state. Moreover, in a given state the treatment may vary over the years, as conventional wisdom changes and the law evolves accordingly. In the absence of specific legislation, the passing of estate property is governed by the existing law at the time of death. A misinterpretation of the law can send you down a fruitless path, so be certain of your facts and up to date on their legal application. I can't emphasize this point enough.

Competent and appropriate counsel should be consulted on all questionable matters.

A probate docket may contain other relevant information and should be examined thoroughly. The thickness of a file may clue you in to a previously existing problem that has been legally addressed and possibly cured. In docket D9/46 you find correspondence leading you to believe that Allison Porter died in March 1990 from injuries sustained in the accident. These purported facts will need to be authenticated by vital records or an official affidavit. Written testimony by family members may be a valid tool in the absence of recorded documents. More often than not, such testimony will lead you to the vital statistics you seek. In order to get the family to supply this information you will need to break the ice with them. The Portland phonebook has a listing for a Jason McCrumb at 1927 Summit Avenue. If for some reason the number is not listed, you could talk to his neighbors, the librarian, town officials, or other locals in an effort to contact him.

Making Contact

A t this point in a project, my heart starts pounding a hole through my chest. There's nothing quite like the emotion of entering the last tunnel in your quest for ownership. There is a place in all successful projects where the fuzzy borders of reality take on definition, your imagination filling in the remaining details, and your enthusiasm, pride, knowledge, and wonder converging in a surge of exhilaration. Time to make contact—or is it?

Before making initial contact with a potential heir, I go through a careful preparatory routine. This includes file organization, legal review, map construction, pedigree charting, and a concise recap display. In the case of our sample lot, from all indications, the one-third interest of Peter Porter in the owner-unknown parcel is held by his daughter Melissa McCrumb, for herself and as guardian of Allan and Annette Porter. The other two-thirds interest is vested in Kevin Tyler of Summerset. By adding the updated information to your existing sketch description or flowchart (Appendices 5 and 6, respectively), you will have a current working model with which to undertake the final phase of the project.

This is an ideal time to examine and rearrange your locus file. The contents, by now probably unwieldy, should all be reviewed, categorized, and refiled into separate folders. Documents dealing directly with the passage of title to the owner-unknown parcel, including all plans, deeds, decrees, and pedigrees, should be retained in the primary file. (If you are working on more than one venture, be sure to label each folder with the project name.) All abutter information, including current assessor's data, should be placed in a new folder, or folders, depending on the volume of material. The bulk of the remaining contents should be divided among three folders marked "Supportive" (testimonies, vital records, historical references, and newspaper articles), "Legal" (statutes, case law, realty trusts, and correspondence with legal counsel), and "Miscellaneous" (sundry leftover and peripheral items). As you rearrange materials it is a good idea to reference each document on the inside cover of the appropriate folder. For each folder, list and arrange the contents chronologically, with date, brief description, book and/or page, and where the document can be found. It sounds tedious, but this practice is a real time- and frustration-saver.

Map construction is a highly efficient and effective visual aid, not only for your own edification but also in communicating with an owner, a lawyer, or title examiner. It is good practice to confirm your title chain before contacting possibly interested parties. When presenting your project, always remember that you have been living with this title and have actually been on the land. Your own maps as well as historical and current assessor's maps can lend striking perspective to sophisticated documents and facilitate negotiations. I use these maps to correlate owner and abutter information with their respective parcels of land. For instance, employing a highlighter, I might identify my locus in yellow, both on the map and in the file folder, and designate the western abutter and its matching file in orange. For added clarity I insert key references to a particular parcel of land within its boundaries on the map.

A complete and neatly transcribed pedigree chart is another superb communication tool (as well as an ice-breaker) that will create a common ground and hopefully put you on a friendlier footing with your new acquaintances. Quinsept Incorporated's *Family Roots*®, software for genealogy enthusiasts, is the program I use for preparing such documents. More often than not, heirs are more interested in their family history than the property left behind. The genealogical tree will be an object of mutual interest and shared knowledge. From the standpoint of the heirs, the gift of hereditary knowledge is priceless, much appreciated, and gratifying. Never underestimate this contribution. Preparing these charts always calls forth the sobering realization that I am more conversant with another family's history than my own.

In communication there is no right or wrong, just what works and what doesn't. It has been my experience in this final phase that as your communication goes, so goes the project. A good technique is to try reversing roles and to visualize yourself being approached by a stranger wishing to engage you in matters of your family history. This is not meant to lock you into a particular agenda or rehearsed conversation, just to help you anticipate the kind of response and exchange you can expect. Being prepared and having your files in hand should give you the confidence to handle whatever comes your way. A friendly and forthright approach, with your purpose clearly stated and no hint of a hidden agenda, will usually generate trust and goodwill, and dispose a stranger to reply in kind.

At this point you are merely looking for an opening, not a signature. Begin with a simple "Hello, my name is Jay Segel from Massachusetts. You don't know me, but I have been studying your family history and its connection with the township of Farmington, Massachusetts." Addressing Melissa McCrumb, I ask, "Are you the daughter of Peter Porter?" Carefully listen to and gauge her response—its manner, tone, and length—and proceed accordingly. For example, if the person is apprehensive, be low-key and reassuring. If she is inquisitive, engage and inform her. Always be polite and show respect. Nothing enrolls people in conversation like enthusiasm, respect, and the open, honest imparting of information that relates to them. In fact, it's downright contagious. Be thorough and complete in divulging information concerning their relatives, and ask for their verification of these facts in an interested, questioning manner so as to elicit complete responses. This is important because people need to serve as well as be served. It is a dialogue worth having regardless of your reason for calling. Often, as happens here, little surprises are unearthed.

It seems that Peter Porter had a third daughter named Roberta, by his second wife Lynn. Melissa also mentions that Lynn died about the same time her father did and that Roberta ran off with a drifter named Paul Bridges. Alluding to her half-sister as "Robbie," Melissa discloses that Roberta left home at the age of 18 and was pregnant at the time, and that no one has heard from her since. These revelations obviously complicate our situation and call into play relevant state statutes to address some important legal questions. In the absence of a will the second wife, Lynn, stood to inherit either a life estate or a state-determined fractional interest per its rules of descent, but only if she survived husband Peter. At the time of her passing, and again in the absence of the decedent's expressed and recorded wishes, any and all interest would pass to the missing daughter. It so happened that Lynn, the second wife, died before Peter, and so all of Peter's interest passed to his three daughters equally. Even though the third daughter was omitted from Peter's probate proceedings she retained the right of inheritance, since the law guarantees a child's inheritance even if an individual is omitted from a will. Children and spouses are referred to as "forced" heirs, and as such they cannot be excluded from an estate, whether mistakenly or intentionally.

Peter Porter's 1/3 interest looks a little different in this context. Each daughter garners a 1/9 interest in the overall estate. Melissa McCrumb retains her portion, and, as guardian, also represents the 1/18 interest vested separately in her niece and nephew, which they received at the time of their mother Allison's death. The remainder of Peter's claim in the owner-unknown land lives with Robbie and/or her heirs. By now you should know what's next. Right, more research. But after a fruitless search in the local archives, you now realize you need other resources.

Other Government Resources and Vital Records

Owner-unknown researchers will find the bulk of the public records they need in town halls and county courthouses. However, in unusual situations or when tracking several individuals over a wide geographical spectrum, it may be necessary or advantageous to resort to broader-based repositories at the state and federal levels. If, after all your local research, you are still stymied by gaps in the record and need additional information or documentation, the state archives should be your first recourse. Some states have two or more facilities that contain public records of importance to the real estate treasure hunter. There may be a separate judicial archive that contains records of court cases, or there may be a state historical society. Since title to land can be conveyed and confirmed by death, deed, or decree, you may find applicable records in the judicial archives and not in the state archives, so check everywhere. A comprehensive list of state archives and record centers can be found in Appendix 10. These institutions should be approached in essentially the same manner as the local facilities already discussed. You never know what pearl you may uncover with an exhaustive search among the voluminous and diverse collection of papers, deeds, letters, manifests, and statistical reports housed there. In some instances, these records may be the only means of discovering missing heirs or determining their whereabouts.

Also at the state level, visit state libraries, notably the state supreme court library. Other than your lawyer's office, this is the best place to become familiar with the intricacies of conveyance law and its precedent-setting cases. Discreet questioning of the support staff followed by a good mental workout at these facilities could save you thousands of dollars in legal costs. Besides operating archives and libraries, state governments also routinely publish a wide variety of studies that may be of interest and may not be available elsewhere. Obtain copies of relevant reports, if you can, and peruse them at your leisure.

Impasses in the owner-unknown search most commonly occur when the last known owner disappears. In these cases the owner usually lives and/or dies out of town, and no probate docket has been found locally. The best way to locate these "missing" persons is through the state department of vital statistics, an official agency in which are deposited statewide marriage, birth, death, and divorce records. A complete and updated list of these bureaus can be purchased for a nominal fee by writing to the U.S. Government Printing Office, Superintendent of Documents, Washington, DC 20402. Ask them to send you Document No. 017-022-00847-5, *Where to Write for Vital Records.* Another approach is to use Thomas Kemp's *International Vital Records Handbook,* which contains blank vital records application forms from every state (published by Genealogical Publishing Company, Baltimore).

You can pursue your search through the mail, but obviously it is to your advantage to visit as many bureaus as you can personally. The idea here is to find the desired probate docket, which is usually only found in the county or town of the state where the person died. Start by checking the home-state death certificate index for evidence of the owner's death, beginning with the year of the last known transaction in which the owner was involved, and carrying the inquiry forward a reasonable amount of time, usually no more than 100 years. If you come away empty-handed, repeat the process for the state containing the locus, then the surrounding states, as needed, until you hit paydirt.

Vital records are the best way to prove lineal relationship, as in the cases of Allison and Robbie Porter. Each of these documents should name the place of birth, death, or residence, along with names of parents, if known. By matching birth and death certificates, this allows for reasonable certainty in establishing family relationships. Robbie Porter's birth record shows Peter Porter as the father, so she stands to inherit a 1/9 interest in the land. Remember, Peter had a 1/3 interest. At his time of death, under the presented circumstances, and in this state, Peter's three daughters split his interest equally, 1/9 each. In the case of Allison Porter, her twins divide her 1/9 share evenly, owning 1/18 each. Her death certificate is necessary to prove that the land could pass. It also offers valuable information that wasn't available elsewhere, like her date of death (3/30/90). The stated place of death, in other cases, could lead you to a missing probate and possibly to more owner-known land. Marital status at the time of death is very important to the passage of title, as was highlighted in the last chapter. Death certificates also note the name of the informant and usually his relationship to the deceased. This can give important clues to missing heirs. A vital records chain from the last known owner to his living heirs is an essential part of any acceptable title outline. In the case of a married daughter, the vital records explain the concurrent name changes on the title by revealing her maiden name and thus her relationship to the previous owner. A parallel, or sibling, relationship can be ascertained through vital records by matching one or more parents. All these family relationships can be presented neatly and concisely by organizing the vital statistics in accordance with the descendancy chart provided for you in Appendix 7.

Federal repositories are another alternative to local facilities. The United States government takes a serious interest in the preservation of American history and heritage, as evidenced by the numerous federally-funded libraries and record centers around the country. Of all these institutions, the best known, perhaps, is the Library of Congress, where one can find a wealth of material on history and genealogy. However, the main government repository, for records dating from the formation of the Republic, is the National Archives and its associated Federal Archives and Record Center (FARC) branches. The bibliography in Appendix 9 includes several sources that furnish guidance on how to use the vast holdings of the National Archives. Appendix 10 lists addresses and telephone numbers of the National Archives and FARC branch offices, while Appendix 11 shows the states serviced by each branch. Among the usual assortment of maps, manifests, deeds, and other documents of interest to the title researcher, these archives contain the most complete set of United States census records, dating back to the first federal census of 1790.

Census information can be crucial in establishing family membership and location, especially when looking for lost heirs or verifying a suspected relationship. Remember, however, that because of privacy restrictions these records are not available to the general public for seventy-two years after the information is gathered and hence have limited value in the case of searches involving more recent heirs at large. The U.S. census has shifted over the years and not merely in terms of population. For background on how census objectives and format have changed with changing times, consult the reading list in Appendix 9 or contact the Bureau of the Census for a complete "fact-finder" kit. (The Bureau is located in Suitland, Maryland, but address all inquiries to the United States Department of Commerce, Bureau of the Census, Washington, DC 20233.) For those who prefer to do business more directly by phone, or on a walk-in basis, you may wish to contact the Census History Staff, Data User Services Division, at their Maryland headquarters.

The United States Department of the Interior, which oversees the Bureau of Land Management (BLM), is a logical resource for landowner information. As of September 1989 there were BLM offices in thirteen western states and an eastern states regional office in Alexandria, Virginia. These offices have a wide variety of research aids, ranging from maps to indexes to U.S. land grants, and are particularly useful in cases where one or more abutters to your owner-unknown parcel is the United States government. For maps and associated data contact also the United States Geological Survey (USGS). One parcel I worked on had a set concrete bound that did not relate to other boundary markers on the property. Closer examination showed it to be an old USGS bound. I called the agency's main office in Reston, Virginia, and after some frustration with employees passing the buck, I found out that this was an elevation marker and received other helpful information. The individual who gave me the scoop was kind enough to send me maps of the area in question. A similar organization you may choose to visit in the Washington area is the National Geodetic Survey, located in Rockville, Maryland.

It is not uncommon to find a foreign-born owner in your title chain. In these cases, you may need immigration or naturalization records to track family and inheritance, especially when the party in question dies intestate and without issue. In most state intestate statutes, the parents, followed by siblings, stand to inherit, and so you will need to contact all of these family members who survive the owner, even if they live in another country. Many owner-unknown lands achieved that dubious status when immigrant landowners died intestate and their holdings reverted to relatives left behind in the old country. So you may need to do some foreign genealogy work. From a documentation standpoint, it is useful to note that immigration and naturalization records are usually acceptable replacements for foreign birth certificates and may be a source for the location of foreign heirs. The United States Immigration and Naturalization Service has amassed an impressive archives of such records and related data and makes the material available for public inspection. If a search of the Service's files proves fruitless, you should check ships' manifests, which can be found on microfilm at selected libraries and local and state historical and genealogical societies.

As we all should remember from grade school, most of this glorious land we call the United States of America was occupied by Indians. In fact, much of this land was conveyed, stolen, adjudicated, or negotiated from their hands and delivered to settlers, servicemen, or the government. Surviving records of these transactions, including maps and deeds, are in the possession of the Bureau of Indian Affairs, Washington, DC. These Native American records may also be found locally if there is still an active tribal council in the area. Where you have specific knowledge, other federal agencies may be helpful in your quest, such as the National Personnel Records Center in Missouri, the U.S. Bureau of Prisons and the U.S. Veterans Administration, both in Washington, DC, and, in Baltimore, the National Center for Health Statistics and the Social Security Administration (SSA). Although the SSA has the largest compilation of employment files in the world, it did not come into existence until the 1930s and hence will be of little use in searches for lost heirs from the 1700s and 1800s. In more recent cases, the social security number itself may provide a valuable clue to an heir's residence, as the first three digits correspond to the issuing state.

Although the On-line Computer Library Center (OCLC) is a private cataloging and networking service sold to libraries, it has numerous government holdings. Moreover, the OCLC is loosely associated with the Library of Congress and provides local online access to many of the Library's documents. It is also the central clearinghouse for the federally-funded United States Newspaper Program and its huge database. The *USNP National Union List* (publication 63a) is a guide to the 77,000 newspapers making up this database. Altogether, the OCLC administers a database containing over 20 million records and some 331 location listings worldwide. The main office is in Dublin, Ohio (see Appendix 10 for address and phone numbers). By requesting a brochure of services, I discovered a handy new research tool called LEGEND, an online database dealing with legal issues. The products and services of the Center are truly astounding. Be advised, however, that one can gain access to LEGEND and the Center's other programs from terminals at participating libraries only. For those obsessive researchers determined to find the most elusive of missing heirs, like Robbie Porter Bridges, it is an indispensable resource. For an OCLC affiliate near you, call the main office in Ohio. They will refer you to the appropriate regional center.

Religious, Institutional, and Business Records

O f all the organizations that conduct, catalog, and propagate genealogical research, undoubtedly the most zealous and meticulous is The Church of Jesus Christ of Latter-day Saints, or Mormons. In every state of the Union there is at least one Latter-day Saint (LDS) genealogical library or family history center. For a complete list of Mormon facilities and accredited genealogists, contact the LDS Family History Library in Salt Lake City, Utah (see Appendix 10 for address). Once you have located the family history center, or "stake," you wish to explore, call ahead, as these facilities are run by volunteers and do not have regular hours.

The family history centers have indexes to the three principal groups of records held in the Family History Library in Salt Lake City: (1) The International Genealogical Index (IGI), with over 100 million names, is a wonderful resource for surname research and is available on microfiche at all the branch facilities; (2) The Family Group Records Archives, arranged alphabetically by the name of the father in each family, contains data on over 8 million families; and (3) The Temple Records Index Bureau (TIB), comprising nearly 40 million cards, is an index to genealogical data gathered from 1842 to 1969. The TIB is not open to the public. However, you can request a search for the particular heir, or heirs, in question. The *International Genealogical Library Catalog* lists the holdings of the various family history centers and is a good place to familiarize yourself with the LDS system.

The Mormons have by far the most comprehensive and sophisticated collection of records outside of government, but most religions have records of interest to the practicing genealogist, which of necessity is what we have become by this point. These ecclesiastical files may lead you to a missing heir's place of death or relocation and therefore his or her probate, if one exists. If you are lucky enough to ascertain the religion of the interested party, be sure not to leave this stone unturned. Records of this type are private, but are usually made available to members of the public who have a legitimate interest. Call ahead so that you're prepared to deal with the guidelines, and present yourself at an appropriate time. Once inside, if your search is unsuccessful, ask for information on other repositories of this religious denomination.

If you haven't found what you are looking for by now, you may be arriving at your last best chance. Among secular sources, medical, hospital, coroner, mortuary, orphanage, school, and prison files comprise the bulk of institutional records. These records can reveal or confirm crucial bits of information, but they presuppose knowledge you would have had to acquire elsewhere. For instance, you may be able to access a decedent's medical files if you know the name of the family physician or the hospital where he or she was pronounced dead, information which is obtainable from a death certificate. Look for the name of the person listed as reporting the death; often it is a relative or neighbor capable of furthering your investigation. Keep in mind that the more recent the records, the more likely they are to be confidential.

Business records work in much the same way as religious and institutional records. These records can pay big dividends, as long as you know the business name and location and can convince the personnel department to grant you access. *The Source,* mentioned earlier, has a good reference guide to companies that keep and share employee information for genealogical purposes. When asking to see these semiprivate records, you must conduct yourself with absolute integrity. Be polite and professional. You may be asked to prove relationship to the party in question or have identification showing your affiliation with a genealogical or historical society before the organization will be willing to cooperate with you. An appropriate degree of persistence may be necessary. A company's indulgence is hard to come by and should be treated as an honor at all times.

A general list of repositories and their holdings, discussed in previous chapters, can be found in Appendix 1. This is a good list to refer to when you think you've tried everything. In checking all these facilities you will have demonstrated thoroughness in your search for missing heirs, documents, and/or maps. You may not find everything that you're looking for, and that's okay, thanks to the problem-solving statutes and the curative procedures underwritten by each state government and dispensed by its lawyers. Remember that a preponderance of evidence in boundary questions and the diligent search for heirs is enough to win most court cases.

Highlights of the Law and Its General Application

A t this point you may feel that we've covered every possible type of record and repository, but there are many more. Still, even by my standards there are limits as to what constitutes an acceptable or reasonable effort, beyond which further exploration becomes torturous and probably futile. Hopefully, you will have found the names and addresses of every interested party. However, even if you have not, do not despair. There remain legal remedies to deal with heirs unknown or unlocated. For the most part, you or your legal representatives must meet the test of having conducted a "diligent search" before resorting to these "curative" methods. If you have kept complete, accurate, verifiable, and easily accessible files, the attorney may not need to duplicate your title work or heir search. Thus, prior attention to recordkeeping could save you a ton of time and money at this point.

Conveyance law is governed by state statute and, for the most part, is thoroughly delineated in every state. These legal guidelines are often challenged, amended, or reversed, as precedents are established and then amended, overturned, or superseded when proven faulty, unjust, or inadequate. I am not a lawyer, and even if I were, it would be impossible to recapitulate every state's conveyance laws within the confines of a single reference guide. I will, however, give you a basic overview, with some practical tips regarding legal counsel, title insurance, and the forms and mechanics of conveyance law.

First, hire a conveyance attorney who is licensed and resides in the state of your owner-unknown locus. If your family or friends cannot suggest such a lawyer, use Appendix 10 to contact the state bar association for recommendations. The status of your lawyer and his/her ability to obtain title insurance are two crucial factors one must consider. You should also discuss money and what you will be receiving in services. I have found that a small retainer, a piece of the action, and a very specific contract nets the best results. Any written contract should include mention of payment arrangements, closing costs, and filing fees. It should clarify responsibility for drawing up deeds and all other requisite forms, and for title and any additional genealogical research. Finally, it should provide specific definition of the owner-unknown locus and a statement as to who is to obtain signatures from the heirs. I suggest that *you* get the signatures. It is also desirable, though not essential, for the attorney to include in the contract a guarantee of marketable title within a specified period.

It is not unusual for a lawyer to request time to deliberate before taking the case. He may require time to review his notes, your requests, and any pertinent files you wish to leave with him. Whether to leave files in the lawyer's custody is a personal judgment call, but, whatever you do, never give up your original records. Personally, I would allow the lawyer no more than two weeks to decide, and I would leave only a basic outline or synopsis of the proposal until presented with an acceptable binding contract. This agreement, or at least a signed statement of intent, should be furnished by the attorney at the next meeting. It is good practice to have your family lawyer or an unbiased attorney review the contract before you sign it.

Assuming that an agreement has been consummated and your new partner is up to speed on the information that you have gathered, a legal game plan must be constructed. As in every game, there are rules (statutes and case law), officials (judges, commissioners, title insurance agents, and registrars), players (all interested parties, including you and your entourage), and a series of challenges to be completed before anyone can win. Proceeding on the premise that all the work on our sample owner-unknown project has been verified by and is acceptable to the legal counsel, you and he will make a final assessment of interest. Simply put, the names and exact percentages of all parties with rights to the property are placed in a title chain. Title and genealogical research are not considered complete until all interested parties with known residence who are alive, lucid, and have not disposed of their property rights have been contacted—in other words, people whose signature will give you interest in the locus, like that of Kevin Tyler.

Interest held in unknown or unlocatable heirs, such as Robbie Porter, will be appropriately dealt with through separate legal processes touched on later in this chapter.

In order to understand the flow of real estate when someone dies in the absence of a will, or dies intestate, you must be familiar with the applicable conditions and rules of descent. As noted previously, even within the same state, land can pass very differently depending on the statutes in place at the time of death. For instance, let's say that an intestate decedent died seized in 1801 and the law applicable at the time states that all property goes to the surviving spouse. Though current statutes give half interest to the surviving spouse and the rest to the children, all rights are held by the surviving spouse, in our example, because of the date of death. Your lawyer's expertise and careful review are very important here. A mistake at this point could net you worthless signatures. As a conveyance specialist, your lawyer may even have a printed model of the rules of descent for your state. Refer to Appendix 12 for a general representation of a rules-of-descent flowchart. If this is not clear, ask your counsel to explain it until you are certain you understand.

Now that we know whom to approach and, potentially, where they are, we need a mechanism of conveyance and an entity to hold the property. When securing interest through deed from an heir, I prefer to be the sole grantee, as opposed to naming all partners in the venture or the corporation I may have formed along the way. I then transfer these rights to a separate entity called a realty trust, an instrument used for its anonymity, precision, and protective features. Your lawyer can prepare such a document, and it must be recorded at the Registry of Deeds or a similar government office. The realty trust documentation should include all of the following elements: a business name, date of commencement, town, county, state, declaration of trust, statement of purpose, schedule of beneficiaries, terms for resignation and appointment, assets, monetary arrangements, and witnessed or notarized signatures of all involved parties. So as not to reinvent the wheel, ask your attorney to provide you with a generic (or "boilerplate") trust. From this template you can personalize a realty trust agreement that is legally acceptable while saving hundreds of dollars in attorney's fees.

The wording of your deed is crucial and should not be left solely to the discretion of your legal counsel. After probing all the deeds that brought you to this point, you must have a pretty good idea of how the document should read. The format I like to follow begins with the name of the grantor, his county and state, then a statement of sale and the consideration (money) paid by the grantee (you, or your realty trust), including the grantee's county and state. On most occasions, the next item would be the specific property description, including plan references, subdivision name, lot number, town, county and state. For the purposes of boundary protection and possibly securing interest to other parcels of land lost by the same decedent, you should add the clause "including but not limited to." Since these deeds are quitclaim in nature, it is appropriate to state that the grantor quits and forever relinquishes all rights, title, and interest to the above-referenced property, for himself, his heirs, and assigns. The deed should finish with a title reference, such as: "For my title see book 131, page 357, at the Squires County Registry of Deeds, Massachusetts, deed dated December 9, 1922, from Joe Johnson to Ralph Porter. Also see probates I-811, Squires County, as well as D1-9854 and D1-9934, Queens County probate dockets, both in Massachusetts."

Now we're just a notarized signature away from partial ownership. When approaching the legal heirs of the owner-unknown parcel, begin with a telephone introduction and, along the lines discussed earlier, engage them in a discussion of their family history. Arrange a meeting within a few days of the phone call and present a copy of their family tree and other interesting artifacts. Explain to them that they may have a fractional interest in a piece of land and that you have spent a great deal of time trying to clear its title. Present the deed, with some type of monetary offer, and tell them that their signature will help you resolve this land's title problem. If they are ready to sign, do it in the presence of a notary public. You should also exchange monies at this time as proof of a valid contract. Avoid such a meeting on Sundays, as it will be hard to find a notary; moreover, some states have "Blue Laws" that may invalidate sabbath transactions.

If the heirs have concerns, listen and respond in a direct and honest manner. If there are questions broached to which you don't know the answer, don't fake it. Instead, say, "I don't know, but I'll find out." Your prompt and thorough follow-through could mean the difference between a signature and an empty-handed exit. If the person needs time to consider the offer, take all your paperwork with you except the genealogy. Check back in ten days so as not to appear pushy, though still keeping the trail warm. After the first signature you can represent yourself to the other heirs as the owner of this tract of "cloudy-titled" land. For the sake of expediency, let's assume that you now have all the interest from Kevin Tyler, Melissa McCrumb, Allan Porter, and Annette Porter, totaling 8/9 interest. The remainder of the residual estate is lost in Robbie Porter. To refresh yourself on the dynamics of the title chain, turn to Appendix 6. Note that the boldface type denotes the interested living heirs.

The last two chapters covered a number of last-resort, alternative repositories for finding unlocated heirs like Robbie Porter. When all of these options have been exhausted and you can't bear to look up the name of Robbie Porter one more time, you'll be glad to know that there are legal remedies for fixing such title defects. Your lawyer will probably want to make a cursory check of your notes and some of the facilities to be satisfied that your search was indeed diligent. At this time the attorney should review with you the remedies for clearing your cloudy title and make specific recommendations as to which method is best under the circumstances.

Equity matters, such as the case of missing heirs or ungarnered interest, are usually settled in the county court system. These proceedings generally require petitions naming the interested parties, their last known address, and a description of the land. Additional paperwork, like appraisals, abstracts (title chains in verbalized legal form), surveys, and appointment of counsel for the defendant(s), called a *"guardian ad litem,"* may be requested to define and protect the rights of minors and unknown or unlocatable heirs. This curative process usually requires direct, receipted mail and public advertisement asking for the named heirs to come forward within a certain time frame or lose their rights to this parcel of land. After the allotted time has passed, and no objections have been filed, the unclaimed interest is usually sold at private auction. This is an action to "quiet" title by adjudication.

The mechanics, time frame, and monetary issues involved in this approach vary from state to state and should be explained to you by your attorney. In some states there are other remedies by adjudication, such as Land Court. Where equity cases deal with the matter of heirs, land courts deal with the boundaries of the locus.

Time is probably the easiest and best known curative procedure for claiming land with a defective title. Every state has provisions for "squatter's rights," or adverse possession. Though this method is relatively slow, it has the virtue of being largely invisible. In the face of difficulties dealing with the heirs-at-law, this may be the least controversial way of clearing a title. Basically, this title-purifying solution involves open, conspicuous, adverse, and notorious use of a parcel over a stated and verifiable period of time, with the occupant accepting responsibility for the local property taxes during that period. So, if someone had an owner-unknown lot fenced in for twenty years, payed the taxes, and met with no recorded objections, he or she, in most states, would be the owner of this land, free and clear. As for back taxes, these are not usually assessed on longstanding owner-unknown parcels, because the levying municipal body never assessed the land or sent the bills.

Although title insurance is not a purifying solution, it is another avenue for bringing partially resolved owner-unknown land to marketability. After verifying the facts with your lawyer, who may also be an agent, the title insurance company could opt to insure over a remote minority interest. The title insurance company could also present you with a policy omitting liability in the matter of specific missing heirs. I recommend against accepting exclusionary types of policies, unless the heirs in question are quite elderly and/or distant. One curiosity to bear in mind regarding title policies is that most companies will insure against parties claiming interest but will not guarantee boundaries. If this is unacceptable to you or your partners, this exclusion may be remedied by a surveyor's written perimeter guarantee.

Sample Case Resolution

I n our sample case, of the several mechanisms available to bring our Massachusetts title to marketability, an equity solution in probate court, called a "petition to partition," turns out to be the optimum method. This method is selected because of the high improbability that Robbie Porter or her heirs or assigns will come forward to claim her 1/9 interest within the state's prescribed time period. To inaugurate the procedure, your attorney files petition to partition papers with the court, including a parcel description, a professional appraisal, a request for the court to appoint counsel to represent unknown or unlocatable heirs, the aforementioned *guardian ad litem,* and payment of any stated filing, mailing, and advertising fees. All of this paperwork is cataloged and filed in a probate docket. Correspondence is then sent to the last known address of the missing heir, with postal instructions to return if not signed for. These letters usually are returned to the court unopened, with return receipt intact, and placed in the partition file. Concurrently, an advertisement is placed in the local paper describing the land and naming the missing heirs. To satisfy the Massachusetts requirement, this article is run the first week in three consecutive months.

With no response filed in our sample case, the court-appointed commissioner for this petition granted our request for a private sale (as opposed to public auction), which was "prayed" for in the petition. The outstanding interest was bought from the court, whereupon we received a commissioner's deed indicating marketable title. Normally, the purchase price is commensurate with the product of the ungarnered fractional interest multiplied by the total appraised value. It is cost-effective for your appraisal to reflect the fact that the locus has a defective title and a missing interest, legitimate complications that should drastically lower the appraised value and hence your purchase price for the ungarnered rights at their sale or auctioning. After expenses, the money is held in escrow by the court for any forthcoming heirs. Should Robbie Porter, her heirs, or assigns challenge our claim after the expiration of the advertised objection period, their remedy is usually limited to the monies received by the court for the ownership share in question, plus the accrued interest.

If an owner being petitioned against, such as a Robbie Porter heir, appears or files an objection within the allotted term, an agreement must be reached. Rights can be bought out or sold out, partially or totally, for money, land, or other valuable consideration, by any of the interested parties. The locus could also be divided and distributed by acreage, creating a true partition. Let us say, for instructional purposes, that our locus is nine acres and all other data remains unchanged, with both parties wanting this land. The lot could be subdivided in the following manner: eight acres for us, and one acre for Robbie Porter or her heirs. This is not a viable solution for small lots like our lot 5 in Pinewood Place, north section, Farmington, Massachusetts. This parcel is diagrammed in Appendix 5, showing the lot as 100 x 120 square feet, or just over a quarter of an acre. Since this tract, by most town standards, is too small to be divided into two building lots, a true partition would create a non-conforming lot with very little value. Before filing a petition for partition, become familiar with the zoning regulations in the area so as not to risk the creation of unbuildable lots based on size or road frontage.

Well, now the land is ours, or is it? If we petitioned the right heirs, we're okay, but if not, title insurance, time, and the land court should protect us. All of these can strengthen a title, though the need for them will vary from case to case. Overall, however, I think you'll find that for a relatively small dollar, title insurance buys substantial peace of mind.

If our sample case were real, this parcel of land would be worth approximately $50,000 to $80,000. Most interests can be garnered for somewhere between $1 and $600, with total legal costs, for a project such as this, amounting to about $2,000. Other miscellaneous expenses such as telephone bills, travel expenses, copying, and other paperwork will bring the total cash outlay to approximately $4,000, although in some court proceedings, or when establishing buildability, you may be asked to survey and/or "perk" test the land, which carries an additional cost of about $750.

All things considered, this scenario demonstrates a handsome return on investment and extra dividends in adventure. Rarely does life present such opportunities! In my home state alone there are three lifetimes' worth of owner-unknown lots to research. True, many of the lots are small, as in our sample case, but there are large parcels as well, with profit potentials running into the millions.

Although project prices will fluctuate with the economy, region, and parcel size, your work will generate equity which can be mortgaged for ready cash. Given the financial dilemma of most would-be homeowners, this equity could be used as a down payment on a house or to fund new construction on this very lot. Alternatively, garnering several parcels of land in this manner could provide privacy, income, and retirement security. Not a bad return for a few hours of fun! Well, maybe it was more than a few hours, and maybe it wasn't all fun, but for me, the treasure is well worth the hunt.

Troubleshooting

I f all has gone well, you are now in a position to sell, swap, or mortgage your land. If things haven't gone quite the way you expected, this is your chapter.

You will not find owner-unknown land in every town. In fact, certain states and regions have a higher propensity than others for disputed or untitled land owing to disparate statutes, historical circumstances, and attitudes of civil servants who administer the land and title system. On balance, the Eastern seaboard seems to be the most fertile territory for real estate treasure hunting. This is a point worth remembering when you are ready to undertake your next project, whether the first was successful or not. Following is a list of the most commonly asked questions and their answers.

Q: *What do I do first?*

A: Pick an area, then visit the town assessor's office.

Q: *The assessor says there is no book or list of lots. What now?*

A: Ask how he keeps track of the landowners and the value of their land. Then ask to see those records. This should be public information.

Q: *Why can't I find any owner-unknown land?*

A: There may not be any. Check all assessor and other records thoroughly for missing lots. If you come up empty-handed, try another town.

Q: *Why can't I identify an owner?*

A: You may need to trace the abutters all the way back. If no reference is made in the official records, check old maps and history books for owner references.

Q: *What if I'm not sure if this land was conveyed?*

A: If you are faced with a vague deed, see where else the lot could be located. Also, run schedules on the questionable grantee to see if he or she conveyed this land with a better description. When in doubt, ask your lawyer.

Q: *How do I find the living heirs?*

A: Probate records usually contain addresses, but if they don't, use the phonebook and start calling around. You might also try the historical and genealogical societies.

Q: *Why won't these heirs sell me their interest?*

A: Most of the time it's a matter of money or trust. If an increased monetary offer doesn't work, you probably haven't given them enough information. If they still don't want to sell, move on to the next heir. You may consider letting your lawyer or his agent try. If you still have no luck, see if these people would like to claim this land. If so, you have a right to be paid for your title and genealogical research, as well as a finder's fee. Finder's fees are usually accepted and regulated by state statute.

Q: *Can this really be done?*

A: Yes!

Note: If you're still having problems I can provide consultancy services on a case-by-case basis. For more information write to:

> Dr. J. D. Segel
> P.O. Box 1076
> Oak Bluffs, Massachusetts 02557

Please include your name, address, and phone number and a brief description of the project for which you are seeking assistance.

Appendices

Appendix 1

Checklist of Major Resources

Source	Chief Records Found
1. Town assessor's office	Locus, maps, abutters
2. Town building inspector's office	Maps, permits
3. Town vault	Tax data, vital records
4. Locus	Landmarks
5. Local library (for locus site)	Background information
6. Registry of deeds	Maps, deeds
7. Registry of probate	Wills, decrees, heirs
8. Historical society (of locus site)	Heirs, land data
9. Bureau of vital statistics	Heir records
10. Town clerk (where heir lived/died)	Heir records
11. Historical society (where heir lived/died)	Heir information
12. Library (where heir lived)	City directory/phonebook
13. Genealogical library	Family trees (of heirs)
14. Cemeteries and cemetery records	Heir data
15. Mormon genealogical libraries (LDS)	Heir data
16. Newspapers, periodicals	Obituaries, history
17. Library of Congress	Maps, manuscripts, books
18. National Archives	Heir data, censuses, ships' passenger lists, military records
19. Local surveyor/engineer	Maps, plans, research
20. State highway department	Maps, owner data
21. State bar association/ legal referral services	Local laws, court data

71

22. Rare book stores	Maps, reference works
23. Funeral parlors	Heir information
24. Immigration and Naturalization Service	Naturalization papers, ships' passenger lists
25. Churches	Vital records
26. Hospitals	Heirs, vital data
27. Bureau of Indian Affairs	Genealogy, land notes
28. Daughters of the American Revolution Libraries	Heirs, lineage records
29. Federal Archives and Records Centers (FARC)	Military records, censuses, ships' passenger lists
30. National Personnel Records Center	Military records
31. Graveyards	Vital data
32. Pilgrim Hall	Genealogy, history
33. Bureau of Land Management	Land accounts
34. Legal and genealogical book publishers	Reference books
35. Institute of Genealogy and Historical Research	Genealogy, history
36. Title examiners and genealogists	Professional search

Appendix 2

PROJECT PHONE LIST   Map/Parcel # _____

Area Name & Lot # _____

Town _____   County _____

County Seat _____

County Clerk   _____

Town Clerk   _____

Town Assessor's Office   _____

Registry of Deeds   _____

Title Examiner's # at Registry   _____

Registry of Probate   _____

Local Historical Society   _____

State Historical Society   _____

State Bureau Of Vital Statistics   _____

Local Library   _____

Specialized Library   _____

State Archives   _____

Previous Owner(s) _____

Last Known Owner _____

Heir Notes _____

Reference _____

Appendix 3

Owner Unknown from A to Z

A. Choose locus from assessor's book or from computerized "owners" list.

B. Locate area on assessor's maps, subdivision plans, and in the field.

C. Find any owner, using old tax records, maps, or abutter research.

D. Find last known owner, verifying by cross-referencing with tax records.

E. Identify heirs, using probates, wills, genealogy, and state laws.

F. In the registries, run grantor schedules on heirs for conveyances.

G. Locate heirs using probates, wills, libraries, and historical societies.

H. Prepare deeds, using a conveyance lawyer, or read conveyance handbooks.

I. Draft realty trust, using a conveyance lawyer, and record this declaration.

J. Get deeds to the locus from heirs, with notarized signatures.

K. Record deeds at the Registry of Deeds in the county of the locus.

L. Prepare abstract with help of a title examiner, lawyer, or handbook.

M. Tie up loose ends, including affidavits, vital statistics, and probates.

N. Survey land; use a locally licensed surveyor/engineer.

O. Pay taxes at local tax collector's office.

P. Obtain title insurance policy; ask your conveyance lawyer about it.

Q. Petition to partition this land if you cannot get a title policy.

R. Get a written appraisal; call a local bank for direction.

S. Take out a mortgage; this helps to establish ownership and value.

T. List land with real estate agent.

U. Review all purchase and sales agreements with your lawyer.

V. Run a credit check on all potential buyers.

W. Sell the land.

X. Put this money in a new account, reimbursing yourself for expenses.

Y. Set aside "tax money," using the remainder to seed the next project.

Z. Begin your next project(s).

P.S. *COPY EVERYTHING!* Reference the source and the project at the top.

Appendix 4

ASSESSOR MAPS

Composite Assessor's Map

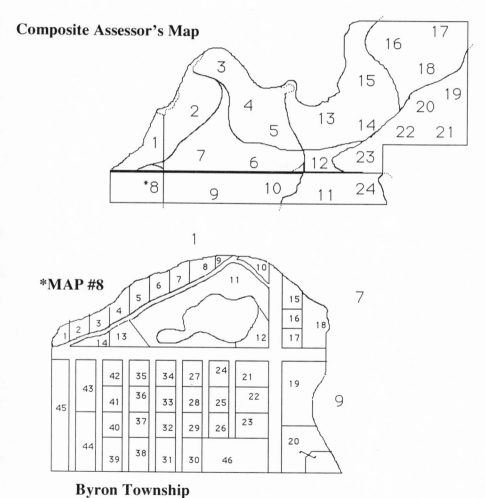

*MAP #8

Byron Township

Appendix 5

SKETCH OF LOCUS FROM DEED DESCRIPTION

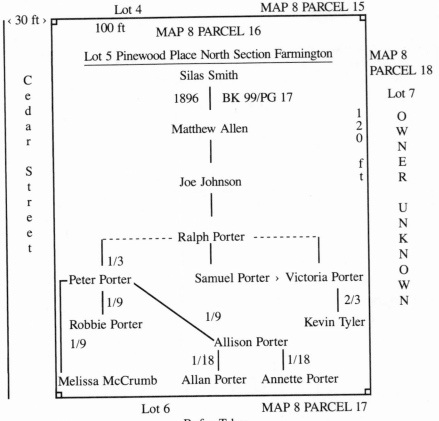

Charles Folger

Lot 4   MAP 8 PARCEL 15

‹ 30 ft ›

100 ft   MAP 8 PARCEL 16

Lot 5 Pinewood Place North Section Farmington

MAP 8
PARCEL 18

Lot 7

Silas Smith

1896 | BK 99/PG 17

Matthew Allen

Joe Johnson

Cedar Street

120 ft

OWNER UNKNOWN

Ralph Porter

1/3

Peter Porter

Samuel Porter › Victoria Porter

1/9

2/3

Robbie Porter

1/9

1/9

Kevin Tyler

Allison Porter

1/18

1/18

Melissa McCrumb   Allan Porter   Annette Porter

Lot 6   MAP 8 PARCEL 17

Rufus Tabor

Pinewood Place Subdivision
Prepared for Silas Smith
Plan # 1119
Farmington, MA
Benjamin Cromwell, Surveyor/Engineer 5/24/1896

Appendix 6

SAMPLE FLOWCHART

Map 8 Parcel 16, Lot 5 Pinewood Place, north section, Farmington, MA

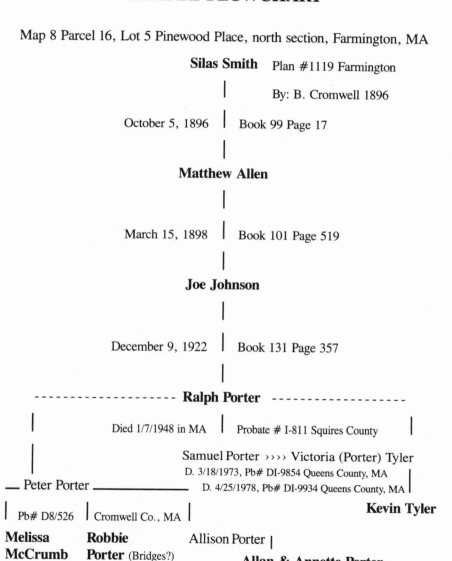

Silas Smith   Plan #1119 Farmington

By: B. Cromwell 1896

October 5, 1896   Book 99 Page 17

Matthew Allen

March 15, 1898   Book 101 Page 519

Joe Johnson

December 9, 1922   Book 131 Page 357

- - - - - - - - - - - - - - - - - - **Ralph Porter** - - - - - - - - - - - - - - - - - -

Died 1/7/1948 in MA   Probate # I-811 Squires County

Samuel Porter ›››› Victoria (Porter) Tyler
D. 3/18/1973, Pb# DI-9854 Queens County, MA
D. 4/25/1978, Pb# DI-9934 Queens County, MA

__ Peter Porter _____

Pb# D8/526   Cromwell Co., MA

Kevin Tyler

Melissa   **Robbie**   Allison Porter |
McCrumb   **Porter** (Bridges?)

Allan & Annette Porter

Appendix 7

DESCENDANCY CHART

GENERATION 1

Spouse #2?
Mother of Sam & Victoria
B
M
D
Pb#

Ralph Porter

B
M
D: 1/7/1948
Pb# I-811 Squires County, MA

Spouse #1?
Mother of Peter
B
M
D
Pb#
Misc: —————————

GENERATION 2

Samuel Porter
B
M
D: 3/18/1973   Pb# DI-9854
Spouse: NONE

Victoria Porter
B
M
D: 4/25/1978   Pb# DI-9934
Spouse: Kevin Tyler
        Pb#: Alive

Peter Porter
B
M: 12/23/1935
D: 6/7/1983   Pb# D8-526
Spouse: Sarah Arey of Odessa, RI
Spouse #2: Lynn?

B
M
D   Pb#
Spouse

GENERATION 3

B
M
D   Pb#
Spouse
Issue

B
M
D   Pb#
Spouse
Issue

Robbie Porter
B: To Peter & Lynn
M
D   Pb#
Spouse: Paul Bridges?
Issue: ?

Melissa Porter
B: 8/25/1939 to Peter & Sarah
M
D   Pb#
Spouse: Jason McCrumb
Issue: NONE

Allison Porter
B: 8/25/1939 to Peter & Sarah
M
D:3/30/1990   Pb# D9-46
Spouse: NONE
Issue: Allan & Annette

80

Appendix 8

Glossary of Terms and Abbreviations

A.K.A.: Also known as (alias)
Abandonment: Informed yielding of one's claim with no future intentions
Abstract: Concise history of real property title
Abutter: Owner of a physically adjacent lot
Access: Ability to gain entrance without trespassing (public or deeded)
Account: A complete fiscal inventory of assets and debits of an estate
Acre rights: Rights of the individual in designated common lands
Acts and resolves: Government statutes with rationale
Adjudication: The final decision of an authoritative body
Administration: Docket of proceedings in settling an intestate estate
Administrator/administratrix (fem): Court appointee handling affairs of an intestate estate
Adoption: Legal creation of relationship (inheritance depends on state and era)
Adverse claim: Land rights based on occupation rather than conveyance
Adverse possession: Ownership after period of open and "notorious" use
Affidavit: Sworn and witnessed statements by parties "in-the-know"
Agent: Employee with power to act on another's behalf
Ancestry: Family history, usually including full names and vital data
Ancient way: Established public access that may or may not be in use now
Appeal: Review of a lower court decision by a higher court of jurisdiction
Appraisal: Valuation used when closing an estate or any other conveyance
Appurtenances: A burden attached to real property, such as an easement
Arbitrator: An impartial, agreed-upon authority to settle a dispute
Archives: Repository of historical records, usually governmental
Assessed value: Municipal appraisal of property used in tax formula
Assessor: Municipal officer dealing with property valuation
Assessor's book: All land and owner data within a certain jurisdiction
Assessor's map: A graphic and numerical referencing of all land in a town
Assets: Anything owned, fully or partially, with monetary value
Assigns: One who gains interest in property through transfer from owner
Attachment: A legal remedy to protect a creditor from a persistent debtor
Auction: Sale, public or private, usually seen in petitions to partition
Authenticate: To prove unrecorded data through supportive documents

81

Award: Final decision of a binding arbitration

Back taxes: Unpaid fee owed to government institution

Bar: Lawyers' association and citizen resource (lawyer referral services)

Bastardy: Verified record of illegitimacy, blood heir born out of wedlock

Beneficial interest: The equitable rights to property held in trust

Beneficiary: Recipient of property, rights, or chattels of a trust or estate

Bequest: Wishes of a decedent as to disposition of his personal estate

Binder: Consideration that creates a temporary contract with assurances

Birth record (B): Authentic document of live birth (town/state vital data)

Blood heir: Direct descendant, omitting adopted relations and spouses

Bk/Pg: Book and page of a referenced transaction, usually at county level

Blue laws: Some states do not honor contracts signed on Sunday

Boilerplate: A standard form, such as a quitclaim deed

Bona fide: An intimation of legitimacy (in good faith)

Bond: Consideration presented to the court by the settler of an estate

Border: A line of demarkation, or adjacent jurisdictions

Bound: A reference marker, usually for separation or elevation

Bounty land: Land given as inducement, used as payment for military service

Brief: Prepared summary of evidence and points of law in a suit

Broker: One who brings together a buyer and seller for a commission

Burden of proof: Verification of allegations by the plaintiff beyond doubt

Cartulary: A register of title deeds and charters

Case law: Corroboration by precedents of verdicts germane to an issue

Caveat: A warning to the buyer (e.g., no guarantee of title marketability)

Census: A comprehensive gathering of specific data, usually related to demography and population

Centennial Digest: Source of reported case law, organized by topic and era

Chattels: All tangible, movable, and personal goods

Citation: Detailed description of a stated fact with reference to source

City directory: Compilation of reference data on residents of a city/town

Civil law: Type of law dealing with rights and duties of persons under contract

Civil action: Suit filed to protect one's contractual rights

Claim: The assertion of a right to assets

Clear title: Ownership of property free from encumbrances (marketable)

Closing: The consummation of a real estate transaction (delivery of deed)

Cloud on title: Impurity of ownership chain to property, usually real property

Codicil: Supplement to an executed will to change, alter, or expand

Comity: Courtesy deferral of a court in concomitant jurisdiction conflict

Commissioner: Court-appointed administrator in probate equity cases

Commissioner's deed: Title from the court after equity case

Common law: System of jurisprudence based on precedent, not statute

Commons: Land set aside, or gifted, for public use

Comparable (comps): Land with similar location and improvements
Composite assessor's map: Numbered layout of every lot in one town
Confirmation: Court acceptance of an arbitration (can apply to title)
Confirmatory deed: A document to correct or clarify a previous recording
Conflicts of law: Two or more statutes creating opposing legal opinions
Conservator: Custodian selected by court to manage property of incapable owner
Consideration: The reason for transferring ownership, usually monetary
Conveyance: Transfer of real property, usually by death, deed, or decree
Conveyance attorney: A lawyer specializing in real property matters
County: State geographical district with a common judicial government
County seat: The "home town" of the county courthouse
Court records: Documents in the Clerk's care (often published)
Covenant: A formal, binding agreement, with promises and/or stipulations
Criminal act: An act done with malicious intent to harm or injure
Curative procedures: Legal remedies to purify a cloudy title
Curtesy: Husband's right to a life estate in all real estate inheritance
Custody: A keeping or caretaking, not ownership
DAR: Daughters of the American Revolution, a very active lineage society
Death record (D): Authentication of death (town/state vital data)
Decedent: One who died "in property" or "died seized"
Decennial Digest: Source of reported case law, organized by topic and era
Declaration of trust: Recorded document creating a consortium with goals
Declaratory judgment: Establishes rights of parties to real property
Decree: A judicial order (can establish ownership or property transfer)
Deed: The most common tool for the transfer of real property
Defunct county: County no longer in existence (absorbed or changed)
Delinquent land: So called when fees or taxes on land become past due
Deposition: Sworn and witnessed statements for pre-trial disclosure
Descendant: Blood heir; heir of the body
Descent and distribution: Disposition of property in an intestate estate
Devise: Expressed wishes of a decedent as to disposition of real estate
Devolve: Passage of an estate by law without intervention
Died seized: Holding title to real property at the time of death
Diligent search: Reasonable examination, not necessarily resolved
Discrepancy: Contrasting assessments arising from vagueness or error
Distraint: Seizure of other's personal property on your land (debt relief)
Distribution: Disposition of personal and real property by will or decree
Division: Fractionalization of real property (town-approved and recorded)
Domain: Ownership of land, immediate and/or absolute
Domicile: The jurisdictional residence claimed as permanent or primary
Dower: Wife's right to a life estate in estate inheritance of land

Easement: A documented right-of-way through real property
Eminent domain: Government method for the taking of land (must pay)
Encroach: An intrusion to unlawfully gain property or authority
Encumbrance: Interest of a third party on property; cloud on a title
Engineer: Certified person who lays out roads, piers, and sewage systems
Environmental controls: Laws to protect fragile ecosystems like wetland
Equity court: Legal remedy to garner outstanding interests
Escheat: The reversion of property to the state (no one else to inherit)
Estate: Interest, right, claim, or possession of land, fully or partially
Et al: Latin for "and others," used in deeds, surveys, and assessments
Et ux: Latin for "and wife," used in deeds, surveys, and assessments
Exchange: Bilateral trading of properties
Execution of instrument: To sign a legally binding deed or contract
Executor: Person making the arrangements for a testate estate
Exhumation: The opening of a grave; usually requires a permit
Extract: Brief direct quote from an authentic record
Extra-legal: Outside of the legal system, not covered by the law
Fair market value: Appraisal based on comparable recent sales
Family group sheet: Genealogical notes on a particular family
Family history center: Local genealogical library affiliated with LDS Church
Family tree: Graphic representation of ancestral lineage
Fee simple: Absolute unencumbered land inheritance of infinite duration
Fee tail: Conveyance setting a fixed inheritance line for succession
Fiduciary: A person having legal responsibility for undertaking an action
Filing date: The date a document becomes public record
Finder's fee: Remuneration given by an owner for lost or unknown treasure
Float a bond: A written monetary assurance allowing time for processing
Flowchart: Historical passage of title with specifics in graph form
Forbearance: A suspension of obligation for a specified period of time
Forced heir: Person who, by law, cannot be disinherited (e.g., children)
Foreclosure: Taking of property for non-performance of contract
Foreign: Different jurisdiction (country or state), e.g., RI will in MA
Freedom of information: A federal act ensuring public record disclosure
Freeholder: Owner of enough land to vote and hold office
Gazetteer: Descriptive guide to geographical features of a specific area
Genealogy: The scientific study of human ancestral succession; the determination of family relationships
General laws: Operating statutes of each state
Geographical index: Ownership cataloged by assessor's map and lot
Gift: Transfer of ownership without consideration
Grandfathered: Exception from non-conformity, based on pre-existence
Grantee: Buyer, inheritor, or otherwise acquirer of property

Grantor: Owner who is selling, willing, or gifting property

Guardian: Appointee who manages affairs for minors or incapable adults

Guardian *ad litem:* Appointee representing minors and/or unknown heirs

Habendum: Clause naming the grantee and limiting the estate being sold

Heir-at-law: One picked to inherit, by statute or will, upon owner's death

Homestead: Primary residence and real estate of the household head

Ibid: Abbreviation meaning in the same way, time, or place

IGI: Internationl Genealogical Index (compiled by the LDS Church)

Improvement: Development or upgrade beyond repair and replacement

Indenture: Conveyance of land by deed, where both parties share duties

Indian claims: Native American rights to land otherwise assessed

In fee: Absolute ownership of real property (used as deed terminology)

Informant of death: Reporter of death, usually a relative (on certificate)

Inheritance: Property acquired from a decedent's estate

Institutional records: Data kept by prisons, schools, orphanages, etc.

Intentions of marriage: Old records of future wedlock announcements

Interest: Provable and enforceable right, not necessarily ownership

Intestate: Dying without a will or with a will that is disallowed or voided

Inventory: An accounting of assets (usually personal and real schedules)

Joint tenancy: Form of ownership with rights of survivorship

Junior (Jr.): Second person in a time period with that name, not always son

Jurisdiction: The power of a court to hear and render a decision

LDS: Latter-day Saints (Church of Jesus Christ of Latter-day Saints), a.k.a. Mormons

Land court: Forum with ultimate jurisdiction over real property

Landlocked: No means of access to a parcel of land without trespassing

Landmarks: Unique/conspicuous physical features (e.g., streams, boulders)

Land records: Documents applying to real estate (e.g., deeds, testimonies)

Land transfer directory: Compilation of conveyances in a certain area

Land warrant: A government guarantee of undisputed ownership

Last known owner: Last party to pay taxes on owner-unknown land

Lawful age: State determination of responsibility for personal action

Legacy: Gift of personal property bequeathed by will

Lien: An attachment on property, usually to settle a debt

Life estate: The ability to live at a premises until death

Like-kind exchange: Swapping investment land for the same (not taxable)

Lineage society: Genealogical organization whose members share similar ancestral history

Link: Surveyor's unit of measure used in the 1800s, equal to 7.92 inches

Lis pendens: A freeze on real property sale because of a pending lawsuit

Locus: The parcel of land in question, the subject of research

Magistrate: A public civil officer with limited judicial power

Manifest: Record of passengers on a ship (immigration data)

Manuscript: An unrecorded or unpublished composition

Marketability: A title that is reasonably free from defects and therefore saleable

Marriage record (M): Certificate of legitimate matrimony (town or state)

Medical records: Records kept by hospitals, doctors, and mortuaries

Metes and bounds: Measurements using landmarks to establish territorial or lot boundaries

Migration: Chartable pattern of population movement

Military records: Documentation of military service and pensions

Misrepresentation: A known false portrayal to achieve personal benefit

Missing interest: Cloudy title or partial ownership

Mortgage: A secured long-term loan contract to buy property, a title lien

Municipality: Local jurisdiction (e.g., city, township)

Naturalization: Process to gain U.S. citizenship for a foreign-born person

Non-resident: Owner living in a state/country other than that of the land

Notary public: Person authorized by the state to verify transactions

Now or formally of (N/F): Labeling of an abutter without present precision

Offer: An overt act of willingness to enter into an agreement

Open and notorious use: Continuous and conspicuous use of real property

Opinion: Supported reason for a point of view or contention using the law

Other valuable consideration: Fee of goods or services in lieu of money

Owner index: Municipal (public) records of owner addresses and valuations

Owner of record: Party who pays the property tax and has some interest

Owner unknown: Property not currently assessed to anyone, or recognized

Para-legal: Assistant to a lawyer (many title examiners are para-legals)

Parcel: A portion of real property or subdivided lot

Pedigree: Ancestral lineage, usually in chart form

Perambulation: Running of lines for surveying and inspection

Personal property: Those goods which are tangible and movable

Petition to partition: Court process to garner outstanding land interests

Plaintiff: Initiator of a lawsuit, party that has been allegedly "wronged"

Planning board: Local governing body concerned with land use

Plans: Generic term for various types of maps and building designs

Plat: A map locating real estate, its abutters, and landmarks

Power of attorney: Document giving one's right of decisions to another

Precedent: Past adjudication germane to an issue at hand (sets legal trend)

Probatable assets: Estates of sufficient worth to adjudicate (state law)

Probate (Pb): The act of dealing with estate matters

Probate court: County court with jurisdiction over estate and related matters

Property tax: Consideration levied on property for municipal services

Proprietors: Owners, usually of a large tract of subdividable land

Public domain: Land owned by the government
Purchase and sales agreement: Contract to transfer ownership for reward
Quiet title: A suit in equity brought to clear title (declaratory judgment)
Quitclaim deed: Conveyance of all rights, title, and interest, if any
Real property: Land and what is attached to it, including its minerals
Realty trust: Legal form of holding real property
Register: A formal and exacting list of subjects with parity for posterity
Registered land: Real property with ownership decreed by land court
Registrar: Elected or selected civic officer in charge of recordkeeping
Registration: A formal and precise recording of documents
Registry: Government, usually county-based, house of records
Relict: Husband or wife who survives the other spouse
Relief: A judgment to establish rights, usually in a court of equity
Religious records: Vital records, baptisms, confirmations, burials, etc.
Removed: Leaving one place to take up residence elsewhere
Renvoi: Looking to the laws of a non-resident's domicile in local conflict
Repository: Place where records are kept
Rescission: To cancel an agreement and return to pre-contractual position
Resident: Person living in the same place as the real property in question
Residuary clause: Phrase in a will that disposes of non-inventoried items
Residuary estate: That part of an estate omitted from an inventory
Resource: A person, place, or thing housing viable information
Rest, residue, and remainder: Non-inventoried property
Restraint on alienation: Restrictions on conveyance of real property
Rights: Individual liberties enforceable by law
Right of redemption: Subject claim to an incorrect civil land-taking
Right of privacy: State law forbidding public access to records
Rights of survivorship: Interest passes at death to other owners
Rod: Antiquated unit of measurement equal to 16.5 feet, used by surveyors
Rule against perpetuities: Unclaimed interest in property has a time limit
Rules of descent and distribution: State laws dictating property passage
Run with the land: The burdens and benefits of land pass with conveyance
Sachem: Indian head of tribal affairs in a particular area
Schedule of beneficiaries: List of those having equity interest in a trust
Scrivener's error: Transcription mistake or omission in a document
Seal: An impression formally attesting to the execution of a contract
Setbacks: Minimum distance one can build to a boundary line (local law)
Settlement of estate: Resolution of all estate matters to court approval
Share: An allotment of property, usually by deed or decree
Signature: A sign of personal acceptance or corroboration
Skeptical data: Unrecorded and unverified information and hearsay
Sovereign: The governing body or jurisdictional controller over property

Squatter's rights: Land rights acquired by occupation over a set period
Statute: Act of legislation, the law governing conduct within its scope
Straw: Deed to a third party for purposes of anonymity
Subdivision numbers: Reference numbers identifying each lot (plat number)
Survey: Precise drafting of a certain tract of land with labeled abutters
Tacking: Using past possession time on cloudy title land for adverse claim
Tax records: Stored data on the tax history of specific lots of real estate
Tax-taking: Municipal taking of land for non-payment of taxes
Tenants-in-common: Ownership where each interest is held separately
Tertia: Third person in a period of time with same name (not always son)
Testator: A person who dies with a court-approved will (maker of a will)
Testimony: A sworn and binding statement (may be made public record)
Title: Recorded certificate of property ownership
Title chain: Derivation of real property and delineation of its transactions
Title examination: Research to uncover flaws in property ownership
Title insurance: Protection bought for undiscovered risks of ownership
Torrens: Land registration system based on tracts and their title chains
Town hall: Local government building housing records and offices of public officials
Township: Local government entity managing local affairs
Transaction date: The date of contract or instrument execution
Trust: An entity holding property for the benefit of others
Trustee: Holder and administrator of legal title for the benefit of others
U.S.G.S.: United States Geological Survey (government mapping agency)
Unregistered land: Real property that has never been decreed by land court
Vault: Walk-in secured storage unit for precious government records
Viable heir: Living heir of last known owner with vested interest
Vital records: Official birth, marriage, death, and, often, divorce records
Voter's list: List of residents, of lawful age, who are registered to vote
Ward: Person and/or property over which the court appoints a guardian
Warranty deed: Conveyance of real property with a vow to defend the title
Wetland: A designated area of ecological fragility, usually unbuildable
Will: Expressed wishes of a person as to the settlement of his/her estate
Without issue: Having no children (important in cases of intestacy)
Witness: One who swears to a contract as written
Zoning: Local laws governing lot size and usage (overseen by a board)

Appendix 9

Suggested Reading and Reference Aids

I have carefully constructed the book list below to provide the real estate treasure hunter with useful information on regional history, sources, research, and document organization. In addition, I've included books which concentrate on specific resources and subject matter. These publications are what I consider the cream of the crop; however, new books are coming out daily, and there are many other titles of great value. Given the nature of this guide, it would be unwarranted and next to impossible to list all relevant publications, though of course one book will inevitably lead you to others. Publishers of reference books cater to the researcher, so request catalogs from all of them; you never know what valuable new sources you might discover! The following are among the most important publishers in the field:

GRC: Gale Research Company, Detroit, MI (313) 961-2242
LCP: Lawyer's Cooperative Publishing, Rochester, NY (716) 546-5530
GPC: Genealogical Publishing Company, Baltimore, MD (301) 837-8271
APC: Ancestry Publishing Company, Salt Lake City, UT (800) 531-1790

Akey, Denise S., ed. *Encyclopedia of Associations,* 24th ed. GRC, 1990.
Anderson, Robert M. *American Law of Zoning,* 3rd ed. 5 vols. LCP, 1986.
ARCO. *America's Phone Book.* Arco, 1989.
Ayer Press. *Ayer Directory of Publications,* 115th ed., 1983 (or current ed.).
Barring, Robert, and Morris Cohen. *How to Find the Law,* 9th ed. West Publishing Co., 1989.
Baxter, Angus. *In Search of Your European Roots.* GPC, 1985.
Bentley, Elizabeth P. *County Courthouse Book.* GPC, 1990.
Black, Henry C. *Black's Law Dictionary.* West Publishing Co., 1990.
R. R. Bowker. *American Library Directory,* 43rd ed. R. R. Bowker Co., 1990-1991.
———. *Sources of Serials,* 2nd ed. R. R. Bowker Co., 1981.
Bureau of the Census. *Age Search Information.* U. S. Government Printing Office, 1990.
Cerny, Johni, and Wendy Elliott, eds. *The Library: A Guide to the Family History Library.* APC, 1988.

89

Cerny, Johni, and Arlene Eakle, eds. *The Source.* APC, 1984.

Dollarhide, William, and William Thorndale. *Map Guide to the U.S. Federal Censuses, 1790-1920.* GPC, 1987.

Eichholz, Alice, ed. *Ancestry's Red Book,* APC, 1989.

Filby, P. William. *A Bibliography of American County Histories.* GPC, 1985.

Friedman, Jack P., Jack C. Harris, and Bruce Lindeman. *Real Estate Handbook.* Barron's, 1988.

————. *Dictionary of Real Estate Terms,* 2nd ed. 1987.

Ganstadt, Edwin S. *Historical Atlas of Religions in America.* Harper & Row, 1962.

Gifis, Steven H. *Law Dictionary.* Barron's, 1984.

Greenwood, Val D. *The Researcher's Guide to American Genealogy,* 2nd ed. GPC, 1990.

Hefner, Loretta L. *The WPA Historical Records Survey.* Society of American Archivists, 1980.

Kaminkow, Marion J., ed. *United States Local Histories in the Library of Congress: A Bibliography.* 5 vols. GPC, 1976.

Kemp, Thomas J. *International Vital Records Handbook.* GPC, 1990.

Library of Congress. *National Union Catalog of Manuscript Collections.* Library of Congress, 1975.

Luebking, Sandra, and Loretto D. Szucs. *The Archives: A Guide to the National Archives Field Branches.* APC, 1988.

Mendler, Edward C. *Massachusetts Conveyancers' Handbook,* 3rd ed. LCP, 1984.

National Archives. *Guide to Genealogical Research in the National Archives,* rev. ed. National Archives Trust Fund, 1985.

National Historical Publications and Records Commission. *Directory of Archives and Manuscript Repositories in the United States,* 2nd ed. Oryx Press, 1988.

Neagles, James. *Confederate Research Sources.* APC, 1987.

Stemmons, John. *U. S. Census Compendium.* Everton Publishers, 1973.

Stephenson, Richard. *Land Ownership Maps.* Library of Congress, 1967.

Tepper, Michael. *American Passenger Arrival Records.* GPC, 1988.

Tompkins, Dorothy. *Court Organization and Administration: A Bibliography.* University of California Press, 1973.

U. S. Dept. of Health and Human Services. *Where to Write for Vital Records.* Government Printing Office, 1987.

Vernier, Chester G. *American Family Laws.* 7 vols. and supp. Stanford University Press, 1931-38.

William Clements Library. *Research Catalog of Maps of America to 1860 in the William L. Clements Library.* 4 vols. G. K. Hall, 1973.

Young, Margaret L., and Harold C. Young, eds. *Directory of Special Libraries and Information Centers,* 6th ed. GRC, 1981.

Appendix 10

Selected Resources by State

Since most of the institutions listed on the following pages are research facilities, I have chosen, wherever possible, to give their actual locations rather than their mailing addresses. Call ahead for policies, fees, and hours.

Alabama   (records begin approximately 1768)

State Law Library   205-242-4347
  Judicial Bldg., 445 Dexter Ave., Montgomery, AL 36130

State Department of Archives and History   205-261-4361
  624 Washington Ave., Montgomery, AL 36130

State Bureau of Vital Statistics   205-242-5033
  Dept. of Public Health, 434 Monroe St., Rm. 215,
  Montgomery, AL 36130

State Land Division   205-242-3484
  64 N. Union St., Montgomery, AL 36104

Birmingham Public Library   205-595-5821
  2115 7th Ave. N., Birmingham, AL 35203

Mobile Public Library   205-438-7094
  701 Government St., Mobile, AL 36602

Institute of Genealogy and Historical Research   205-870-2749
  800 Lakeshore Dr., Samford University Library,
  Birmingham, AL 35229

Historical Association   205-324-0998
  3121 Carlisle Rd., Birmingham, AL 35213

Bar Headquarters   205-269-1515
  415 Dexter Ave., P.O. Box 671, Montgomery, AL 36104

Alaska   (records begin approximately 1802)

State Library   907-465-2910
  State Office Bldg., Box G, Juneau, AK 99811

State Archives   907-465-2275
  141 Willoughby Ave., Pouch C-0207, Juneau, AK 99811

Federal Archives and Records Center   907-271-2441
  Federal Office Bldg., 654 W. Third Ave., Rm. 012, Anchorage, AK

Elmer E. Rasmuson Library   907-474-7481
  University of Alaska, Fairbanks, AK 99701

State Court Library   **907-264-0586**
303 K St., Anchorage, AK 99501

Historical Library   **907-465-2925**
Division of State Libraries, Pouch C, 333 Willoughby Ave.,
Juneau, AK 99811

Bureau of Vital Statistics   **907-264-0692**
Dept. of Health and Social Services, P.O. Box H, Juneau, AK 99811

Historical Society   **907-276-1596**
524 W. 4th Ave., Anchorage, AK 99501

Bureau of Land Management   **907-271-5555**
222 W. 7th Ave., No. 13, Anchorage, AK 99513-7599

Bar Association   **907-272-7469**
310 K St., No. 602/Box 100279, Juneau, AK 99501

Arizona   (records begin approximately 1631)

State Archives and Library   **602-225-4159/256-6372**
1700 W. Washington/Third Floor, State Capitol, Phoenix, AZ 85007

State Highway Plans   **602-255-7498**
1655 W. Jackson, Rm. 112, Phoenix, AZ 85007

Vital Records Section   **602-542-1080**
Arizona Dept. of Health Services, P.O. Box 3887, Phoenix, AZ 85030

Historical Society   **602-255-4479**
1242 N. Central Ave., Phoenix, AZ 85201

Bureau of Land Management   **602-241-5504**
3707 N. 7th St./P.O. Box 16563, Phoenix, AZ 85011

U.S. Court of Appeals   **602-379-3879**
230 N. First Ave., Phoenix, AZ 85025

Bar Association   **602-252-4804**
363 N. First Ave., Phoenix, AZ 85003

Arkansas   (records begin approximately 1815)

State Library   **501-682-1527**
1 Capitol Mall, Little Rock, AR 72201

Historical Association, History Department   **501-575-3001**
12 Ozark Hall, University of Arkansas, Fayetteville, AR 72701

Historical Commission   **501-371-2141**
1 Capitol Mall, Little Rock, AR 72201

Division of Vital Records   **501-661-2336**
Dept. of Health, 4815 W. Markham St., Little Rock, AR 72205

Arkansas Supreme Court Library   **501-682-2147**
Justice Bldg., 625 Marshall St., Little Rock, AR 72201

Bar Association   **501-375-4605**
400 W. Markham St., Little Rock, AR 72205-3867

California (records begin approximately 1773)

State Library, Sutro Branch   415-731-4477
480 Winston Dr., San Francisco, CA 94132

State Archives   916-445-4293
1020 O St., Sacramento, CA 95814

Genealogical Research Center   415-558-3191
San Francisco Public Library, Civic Center, San Francisco, CA 94102

State Law Library (Library and Courts Bldg.)   916-445-4027
914 Capital Mall, Box 2037, Sacramento, CA 95809

Henry E. Huntington Library   818-405-2275
1151 Oxford Rd., San Marino, CA 91108

Federal Archives and Records Center   415-876-9009
1000 Commodore Dr., San Bruno, CA 94066

Federal Archives and Records Center   714-643-4241
24000 Avila Rd., Laguna Niguel, CA 92677

State Bureau of Vital Statistics   916-445-2684
Dept. of Health Services, 410 N St., Sacramento, CA 95814-4381

Chinese Historical Society   415-391-1188
17 Adler Place, San Francisco, CA 94133

Society of California Pioneers Library   415-861-5278
456 McAllister, San Francisco, CA 94102

Southern California Genealogical Society Library   818-843-7247
122 S. San Fernando Blvd./Box 4377, Burbank, CA 91503

Historical Society   415-567-1848
2090 Jackson St., P.O. Box 44327, San Francisco, CA 94109

Los Angeles Public Library   213-612-3200
630 W. 5th St., Los Angeles, CA (temp. site: 433 S. Spring St.) 90071

Immigrant Genealogical Library   818-848-3122
1310 W. Magnolia Blvd., Burbank, CA 95128

Bureau of Land Management   916-978-4746
2800 Cottage Way, E-2841, Sacramento, CA 95825

Bar Association   415-561-8200
555 Franklin, San Francisco, CA 94102

Colorado (records begin approximately 1855)

Supreme Court Library   303-861-1111
State Judicial Bldg., 2 E. 14th Ave., B-112, Denver, CO 80203

State Archives   303-866-2055
1313 Sherman St., Denver, CO 80203

Federal Archives and Records Center   303-776-0817/0804
Building 48, Denver Federal Center, Denver, CO 80225

Vital Records Section   303-320-8474
Dept. of Health, 4210 E. 11th Ave., Rm. 100,
Denver, CO 80220-3786

State Historical Society 303-866-2305
Stephen Hart Library, 1300 Broadway, Denver, CO 80203

Denver Public Library 303-571-2000
1357 Broadway, Denver, CO 80203

State Division of Highways 303-757-9220
4340 E. Louisiana Ave., Rm. L-203, Denver, CO 80222

Bureau of Land Management 303-236-1700
2850 Youngfield St., Lakewood, CO 80215

Bar Association 303-860-1115
No. 950, 1900 Grant St., Denver, CO 80203

Connecticut (records begin approximately 1631)

State Law and Legislative Reference Unit 203-566-4601
231 Capitol Ave., Hartford, CT 06115

State Library and Archives archives: 203-566-3690
231 Capitol Ave., Hartford, CT 06115 library: 203-566-4301

Vital Records Section 203-566-2334
Division of Health Statistics, 150 Washington St., Hartford, CT 06106

Historical Society 203-236-5621
1 Elizabeth St., Hartford, CT 06105

Wadsworth Atheneum 203-278-2670, ext 341
600 Main, Hartford, CT 06103

Episcopal Diocese of Connecticut Archives 203-233-4481
Asylum Ave., Hartford, CT 06105

Yale University, Sterling Memorial Library 203-436-8638
120 High St., New Haven, CT 06520

Bar Association 203-721-0025
101 Corporate Place, Rocky Hill, CT 06067

Delaware (records begin approximately 1682)

State Division of Libraries 302-736-4748
43 S. Dupont Hwy., Dover, DE 19901

State Archives 302-736-5318
Hall of Records, Dover, DE 19901

State Bureau of Vital Statistics 302-736-4721
Division of Public Health, Box 637, Dover, DE 19903-0637

Historical Society 302-655-7161
505 Market Street Mall, Wilmington, DE 19801

State Law Library 302-736-5467
Court House, Dover, DE 19901

Rockwood Museum Research Archives 302-571-7776
610 Shipley Rd., Wilmington, DE 19809

Bar Association 302-658-5278
706 Market Street Mall, Wilmington, DE 19801

District of Columbia   (records begin 1790)

National Archives and Records Center	**202-523-3204**
8th St. and Pennsylvania Ave., N.W., Washington, DC 20408	
Library of Congress	**202-707-5000**
Independence Ave. and 1st St., S.E., Washington, DC 20540	
Daughters of the American Revolution Library	**202-628-1776/**
1776 D St., N.W., Washington, DC 20006	**879-3229**
Vital Records Branch	**202-727-5314**
425 I St., N.W., Rm. 3007, Washington, DC 20001-2585	
Society of the Cincinnati Library	**202-785-2040**
2118 Massachusetts Ave., Washington, DC 20008	
Otis Historical Archives	**202-576-2334**
Alaska Ave. and 14th St., N.W., Washington, DC 20306	
Smithsonian Institute Libraries	**202-357-2414**
Constitution Ave. and 10th St., N.W., Washington, DC 20506	
American Bar Association	**202-331-2207**
1800 M St., N.W., Washington, DC 20036	
Howard University Research Center	**202-636-7480**
500 Howard Place, N.W., Washington, DC 20059	
American Library Association	**202-547-4440**
110 Maryland Ave., N.E., Washington, DC 20002	
Marriage Bureau	**202-879-4840**
515 5th St., N.W., Washington, DC 20001	
Bureau of Land Management	**202-343-3193**
451 7th St., S.W., Washington, DC 20240	
Immigration and Naturalization Service	**202-633-2000**
425 Eye St., N.W., Washington, DC 20536	
Folger Shakespeare Library	**202-544-4600**
201 E. Capitol St., S.E., Washington, DC 20003	
Bureau of Indian Affairs	**202-343-1710**
18th and C Sts., N.W., Washington, DC 20245	
U.S. Government Printing Office	**202-783-3238**
Washington, DC 20402	
Veterans Administration	**202-233-4000**
810 Vermont Ave., N.W., Washington, DC 20420	
Social Security Research	**202-282-7206**
4301 Connecticut Ave., N.W., Rm. 205, Washington, DC 20008	
Bar Association	**202-331-3883**
1707 L St., N.W., 6th Floor, Washington, DC 20036	

Florida   (records begin approximately 1764)

State Library, Supreme Court	**904-488-8919**
Supreme Court Bldg., Tallahassee, FL 32399	

State Archives   **904-487-2073**
R. A. Gray Bldg., Pensacola and Bronough St., Tallahassee, FL 32399

Office of Vital Statistics   **904-359-6902**
P.O. Box 210, Jacksonville, FL 32231-0042

Historical Society   **813-974-3815**
University of South Florida Library/Box 290197, Tampa, FL 33687

Tampa (Hillsborough County) Public Library   **813-223-8945**
900 N. Ashley St., Tampa, FL 33602

Orlando (Orange County) Public Library   **407-425-4694**
101 E. Central Blvd., Orlando, FL 32801

Jacksonville Public Library   **904-630-2665**
122 N. Ocean St., Jacksonville, FL 32202

Bar Association   **904-222-5286**
650 Apalachee Pky., Tallahassee, FL 32399-2300

Georgia   (records begin approximately 1733)
State Library   **404-656-3468**
301 Judicial Bldg., 40 Capitol Square, Atlanta, GA 30334

State Archives   **404-656-2393**
330 Capitol Ave., Atlanta, GA 30334

Federal Archives and Records Center   **404-763-7477**
1557 St. Joseph Ave., East Point, GA 30344

State Bureau of Vital Statistics   **404-656-7456**
47 Trinity Ave., S.W., Rm. 217-H, Atlanta, GA 30334-1201

Atlanta Historical Society   **404-261-1837**
3101 Andrews Dr., N.W., Atlanta, GA 30305

Atlanta Public Library   **404-730-1700**
1 Margaret Mitchell Square, N.W., Atlanta, GA 30303

Georgia Historical Society   **912-651-2128**
501 Whitaker St., Savannah, GA 31499

Bar Association   **404-527-8700**
800 The Hurt Bldg., S.E., Atlanta, GA 30303

Hawaii   (records begin approximately 1844)
State Archives and Library   **808-548-2355/4775**
Iolani Palace Grounds, 478 S. King St., Honolulu, HI 96813

Daughters of the American Revolution Library   **808-949-7256**
1914 Makiki Heights Dr., Honolulu, HI 96822

State Bureau of Vital Statistics   **808-548-5819**
Dept. of Health, P.O. Box 3378, Honolulu, HI 96801

Hawaii Chinese History Center Library   **808-521-5948**
111 N. King St., Rm. 410, Honolulu, HI 96817

Supreme Court Law Library   **808-548-7434**
Box 779, Honolulu, HI 96808

Historical Society   **808-537-6271**
560 Kawaiahao St., Honolulu, HI 96813

Bar Association   **808-537-1868**
1001 Bishop St., Suite 950, Pacific Tower, Honolulu, HI 96813

Idaho (records begin approximately 1867)

State Library   **208-334-2150**
325 W. State St., Boise, ID 83702

State Archives   **208-334-3356**
610 N. Julia Davis Dr., Boise, ID 83702

State Vital Statistics   **208-334-5976**
450 W. State St., Boise, ID 83720-6056

Department of Lands   **208-334-3284**
State Capitol Bldg., Rm. 121, Boise, ID 83720

Real Estate Commission Library   **208-334-3285**
633 N. Fourth, State House Mail, Boise, ID 83720

State Historical Society   **208-334-3356**
610 N. Julia Davis Dr. (mailing address)/325 W. State,
Boise, ID 83702

Bureau of Land Management   **208-334-1771**
3380 Americana Terrace, Boise, ID 83706

Bar Association   **208-342-8958**
204 W. State St./P.O. Box 895, Boise, ID 83701

Illinois (records begin approximately 1805)

State Library   **217-782-2994**
Centennial Bldg., Rm. 275, Springfield, IL 62756

State Archives   **217-782-4682**
Archives Bldg., Capitol Complex, Springfield, IL 62756

National Association of Realtors Library   **312-329-8292**
430 N. Michigan Ave., Chicago, IL 60611

NAES College Library   **not listed**
2838 W. Peterson, Chicago, IL 60653

Chicago Bar Association Library   **312-782-7348**
29 S. LaSalle St., Chicago, IL 60603

Center for Research Libraries   **312-955-4545**
6050 S. Kenwood Ave., Chicago, IL 60637

Federal Archives and Records Center   **312-353-0162**
7358 S. Pulaski Rd., Chicago, IL 60629

Newberry Library   **312-943-9090**
60 W. Walton St., Chicago, IL 60610

State Bureau of Vital Records   **217-782-6553**
605 W. Jefferson St., Springfield, IL 62707-5035

Chicago Historical Society   **312-642-4600**
1601 N. Clark St., Chicago, IL 60614

State Historical Society   217-782-4836
Old State Capitol Plaza, Springfield, IL 62701

Bar Association   217-525-1760
424 S. 2nd, Springfield, IL 62701

Indiana   (records begin approximately 1799)

State Library   317-232-3675
140 N. Senate Ave., Indianapolis, IN 46204

State Historical Bureau   317-232-2535
140 N. Senate Ave., Indianapolis, IN 46204

Division of Vital Records   317-633-0274
Board of Health, Box 1964, 1330 W. Michigan,
Indianapolis, IN 46206

State Historical Society   317-323-1879
315 W. Ohio St., Indianapolis, IN 46202

Allen County (Fort Wayne) Public Library   219-424-7241
900 Webster St./P.O. Box 2270, Fort Wayne, IN 46801

Indiana Supreme Court Library   317-232-2557
316 State House, Indianapolis, IN 46204

Jasper Publishing Library   812-482-2712
116 Main St., Jasper, IN 47546

Bar Association   317-639-5465
230 E. Ohio St., 4th Floor, Indianapolis, IN 46204

Iowa   (records begin approximately 1815)

State Library and Archives   515-281-4118/records: 274-2844
E. 12th and Grand Ave., Des Moines, IA 50319

Iowa Genealogical Society Library   515-276-0287
6000 Douglas Ave., Suite 145, P.O. Box 7735, Des Moines, IA 50322

State Bureau of Vital Statistics   515-281-4944
Dept. of Health, Lucas State Office Bldg., Des Moines, IA 50319-0075

State Historical Society   515-281-5111
Capitol Complex, 600 E. Locust, Des Moines, IA 50319

Bar Association   515-243-3179
1101 Fleming Bldg., Des Moines, IA 50309

Kansas   (records begin approximately 1854)

State Library   913-296-3296
State Capitol Bldg., 3rd Floor, Topeka, KS 66612

State Office of Vital Statistics   913-296-1400
Landon State Office Bldg., 900 S.W. Jackson, Topeka, KS 66612-1290

U.S. Bureau of Census   316-231-7100
Dept. of Commerce, 1600 N. Walnut, Pittsburg, KS 66762

Kansas Supreme Court Library   913-296-3257
301 W. 10th St., Topeka, KS 66612

State Historical Society Library   **913-296-4776**
    120 W. 10th St., Topeka, KS 66612

Bar Association   **913-234-5696**
    1200 S.W. Harrison, Topeka, KS 66612

Kentucky   (records begin approximately 1779)

State Law Library   **502-564-4848**
    State Capitol, Rm. 200, Frankfort, KY 40601

State Archives   **502-875-7000**
    300 Coffee Tree Rd./Box 537, Frankfort, KY 40602

State Department of Vital Statistics   **502-564-4212**
    275 E. Main St., Frankfort, KY 40621

Historical Society   **502-564-3016**
    300 W. Broadway/P.O. Box H, Frankfort, KY 40602

Louisville Free Public Library   **502-561-8600**
    301 York St., Louisville, KY 40203

Sons of the American Revolution   **502-589-1776**
    1000 S. Fourth St., Louisville, KY 40203

Bar Association   **502-564-3795**
    W. Main at Kentucky River, Frankfort, KY 40601

Louisiana   (records begin approximately 1769)

State Library   **504-342-4923**
    760 Riverside Mall/P.O. Box 131, Baton Rouge, LA 70821

State Archives   **504-922-1206**
    3851 Essen Lane/P.O. Box 94125, Baton Rouge, LA 70804

State Transportation Surveying Department   **504-379-1131**
    1201 Capitol Access Rd., Baton Rouge, LA 70802

State Vital Records   **504-568-5152**
    P.O. Box 60630, New Orleans, LA 70160-0630

State Historical Society   **504-523-4662**
    533 Royal St., New Orleans, LA 70130

New Orleans Public Library   **504-596-2550**
    219 Loyola Ave., New Orleans, LA 70140

East Baton Rouge Parish Library   **504-389-3360**
    7711 Goodwood Blvd., Baton Rouge, LA 70806

Bar Association   **504-566-1600**
    601 St. Charles Ave., New Orleans, LA 70130

Maine   (records begin approximately 1622)

State Library   **207-289-5600**
    LMA Bldg., State House, Station 64, Augusta, ME 04333

State Archives   **207-289-5790**
    State Capitol, Augusta, ME 04333

State Bureau of Vital Statistics   **207-289-3184**
221 State St., State House, Station 11, Augusta, ME 04333-6831

Historical Society Library   **207-774-1822**
485 Congress St., Portland, ME 04101

State of Maine Law Library   **207-289-1600**
State House, Station 43, Augusta, ME 04333

Bar Association   **207-623-7523**
124 State St./P.O. Box 788, Augusta, ME 04330

Maryland   (records begin approximately 1633)

State Law Library   **301-974-3395**
361 Rowe Blvd., Annapolis, MD 21401

State Archives   **301-974-3915**
Hall of Records, 350 Rowe Blvd., Annapolis, MD 21401

State Bureau of Vital Statistics   **301-225-5988**
4201 Patterson Ave./P.O. Box 68760, Baltimore, MD 21215

Enoch Pratt Free Library   **301-396-5430**
400 Cathedral St., Baltimore, MD 21201

State Historical Society   **301-685-3750**
201 W. Monument St., Baltimore, MD 21201

National Geodetic Survey   **301-443-8631**
N/CG17X2 Rockwall Blvd., Rm. 24, NOAA, Rockville, MD 20852

National Center for Health Statistics   **301-436-8500**
3700 E. West Hwy., Rm. 157, Hyattsville, MD 20782

National Archives and Records Center   **301-763-7000**
4205 Suitland Rd., Suitland, MD 20409

Bureau of the Census Library   **301-763-5042/ data service: 7936**
Federal Bldg. No. 3, Rm. 2449, Washington, DC 20233

Jewish Historical Society   **301-732-6400**
15 Lloyd St., Baltimore, MD 21202

Social Security Administration Library   **301-965-6108**
Altmeyer Bldg., Rm. 571, 6401 Security Blvd., Baltimore, MD 21235

Bar Association   **301-685-7878**
520 W. Fayette St., Baltimore, MD 21201

Massachusetts   (records begin approximately 1620)

State Library   reference: **617-727-2590**/news and periodicals: **2594**
341 State House, Boston, MA 02133

State Archives at Columbia Point   **617-727-2816**
220 Morrissey Blvd., Boston, MA 02125

Boston Public Library   **617-536-5400**
Copley Square, 666 Boylston St., Box 286, Boston, MA 02117

New England Historic Genealogical Society   **617-536-5740**
101 Newbury St., Boston, MA 02116

Massachusetts Historical Society   **617-536-1608**
1154 Boylston St., Boston, MA 02215

Federal Archives and Records Center   **617-647-8104**
380 Trapelo Rd., Waltham, MA 02154

Land Court   **617-227-7470**
Pemberton Square, Boston, MA 02108

The Bostonian Society   **617-720-1713/3285**
15 State St., Boston, MA 02109

Judicial Archives (court records)   **617-725-8044**
1300 New Courthouse, Boston, MA 02108

Pilgrim Hall Museum   **508-746-1620**
75 Court St., Plymouth, MA 02360

Harvard University (Widener) Library   **617-495-2411**
Harvard Yard, Cambridge, MA 02138

Yenching Institute   **617-495-2756**
2 Divinity Ave., Rm. 120, Harvard University, Cambridge, MA 02138

Boston Athenaeum   **617-227-0270**
10½ Beacon St., Boston, MA 02108

Military Records   **617-727-2964**
100 Cambridge St., Boston, MA 02202

Bureau of Vital Statistics   **617-727-8200**
150 Tremont St., Rm. B-3, Boston, MA 02111

American Jewish Historical Society   **617-891-8110**
2 Thornton Rd., Waltham, MA 02154

American Antiquarian Society   **508-755-5221**
185 Salisbury St., Worcester, MA 01609

Bar Association   **617-542-3602/referral service: 9103**
20 West St., Boston, MA 02111

Michigan   (records begin approximately 1796)
State Library   **517-373-5400/law: 0630**
717 W. Allegan/P.O. Box 30007, Lansing, MI 48918

State Archives   **517-373-1408/ genealogy: 1390**
717 W. Allegan, Lansing, MI 48918

Detroit Public (Burton Historical) Library   **313-833-1000**
5201 Woodward Ave., Detroit, MI 48202

Real Estate Division (land records)   **517-373-1250**
Dept. of Natural Resources, P.O. Box 30028, Lansing, MI 48909

State Bureau of Vital Statistics   **517-335-8655**
Dept. of Health, 3423 N. Logan St./P.O. Box 30035,
Lansing, MI 48909

Dissertation Publishing/University Microfilms   **800-521-3042**
300 N. Zeeb Rd., Box 1467, Ann Arbor, MI 48106

Historical Society   **313-769-1828**
2177 Washtenaw Ave., Ann Arbor, MI 48104

Bar Association   **517-372-9030**
306 Townsend St., Lansing, MI 48933

Minnesota (records begin approximately 1831)

State Law Library   **612-296-2775**
117 University Ave., Ford Bldg., St. Paul, MN 55155

State Archives   **612-296-6126**
1500 Mississippi St., St. Paul, MN 55101

Bureau of Vital Statistics, Health Dept.   **612-623-5120**
717 Delaware St., S.E./P.O. Box 9441, Minneapolis, MN 55440

Historical Society   **612-296-6980/2143**
690 Cedar St., St. Paul, MN 55101

American Swedish Institute   **612-871-4907**
2600 Park Ave., Minneapolis, MN 55407

Far Eastern Research Library   **612-926-6887**
5812 Knox Ave. S./P.O. Box 19324, Minneapolis, MN 55419

Immigrant Archives   **612-627-4208**
University of Minnesota, 826 Berry St., Minneapolis, MN 55114

Bar Association   **612-333-1183**
430 Marquette Ave., Suite 403, Minneapolis, MN 55401

Mississippi (records begin approximately 1767)

State Library   **601-359-1036/law: 3672**
1221 Ellis Ave./P.O. Box 10700, Jackson, MS 39209

State Archives and History Dept.   **601-359-6850**
100 S. State St./P.O. Box 571, Jackson, MS 39205

Vital Records Office, State Dept. of Health   **601-960-7450**
2423 N. State St./P.O. Box 1700, Jackson, MS 39205

Historical Society   **601-354-6218**
100 S. State St., Jackson, MS 39205

Northeastern Regional Library   **601-287-7311**
1023 Fillmore, Corinth, MS 38834

Bar Association   **601-948-4471**
643 N. State St./P.O. Box 2158, Jackson, MS 39202

Missouri (records begin approximately 1793)

State Library   **314-751-3615**
2002 Missouri Blvd./P.O. Box 387, Jefferson City, MO 65109

State Archives   **314-751-3280**
1001 Industrial Dr./Box 778, Jefferson City, MO 65102

Natural Resources, Geology and Land Survey   **314-364-1752**
111 Fairgrounds Rd./P.O. Box 250, Rolla, MO 65401

Federal Archives and Records Center   **816-926-6934**
2312 E. Bannister Rd., Kansas City, MO 64131

State Bureau of Vital Records   **314-751-6400**
Dept. of Health, P.O. Box 570, Jefferson City, MO 65102-0570

State Historical Society, c/o University of Missouri   **314-882-7083**
1020 Lowry St., 3 Ellis Library, Columbia, MO 65201

Thomas Jefferson Library   **314-634-2464**
214 Adams St./P.O. Box 89, Jefferson City, MO 65101

Supreme Court Library   **314-751-2636**
Supreme Court Bldg., Jefferson City, MO 65101

Heart of America Genealogical Library   **816-221-2685**
311 E. 12th St., Kansas City, MO 64106

Historical Society of St. Louis   **314-454-3130**
Jefferson Memorial Bldg., Forest Park, St. Louis, MO 63112

National Personnel Records Center (Military)   **314-263-3901**
9700 Page Blvd., St. Louis, MO 63132

National Personnel Records Center (Civilian)   **314-425-5761**
111 Winnebago, St. Louis, MO 63118

U.S. Geological Survey   **314-341-0851**
1400 Independence Rd., Rolla, MO 65401

Bar Association   **314-635-4128**
326 Monroe, Jefferson City, MO 65102

Montana   (records begin approximately 1867)
State Library   **406-444-3115**
1515 E. Sixth Ave., Helena, MT 59620

Bureau of Vital Statistics   **406-444-2614**
Dept. of Health and Environmental Sciences, Cogswell Bldg.,
Rm. C-118, Helena, MT 59620

State Historical Society   **406-444-2681**
225 N. Roberts St., Helena, MT 59620

Missoula Public Library   **406-721-2665**
301 E. Main, Missoula, MT 59802

State Law Library   **406-444-3660**
Justice Bldg., 215 N. Sanders, Helena, MT 59620

Bureau of Land Management   **406-255-2913**
222 N. 32nd St./P.O. Box 36800, Billings, MT 59107

Bar Association   **406-442-7660**
46 N. Last Chance Gulch, Suite 2A, P.O. Box 577, Helena, MT 59601

Nebraska   (records begin approximately 1854)
State Law Library   **402-471-2045**
1420 P St., Lincoln, NE 68508

State Archives   **402-471-4771**
1500 R St., Lincoln, NE 68501

State Surveyor's Office   **402-471-2566**
555 N. Cotner Blvd., Lincoln, NE 68508

State Bureau of Vital Statistics   **402-471-2871**
301 Centennial Mall S., P.O. Box 95007, Lincoln, NE 68509

State Historical Society   **402-471-3270**
1500 R St./Box 82554, Lincoln, NE 68501

American Historical Society   **402-474-3363**
631 D St., Lincoln, NE 68502

Daughters of the American Revolution Library   **308-381-5333**
211 N. Washington St., Grand Island, NE 68801

Bar Association   **402-475-7091**
635 S. 14th St., Hruska Law Center, Lincoln, NE 68508-5007

Nevada   (records begin approximately 1851)

State Library and Archives   **702-885-5160/law: 5140**
Capitol Complex, 401 N. Carson St., Carson City, NV 89710

Division of Archives and Records   **702-687-5210**
Capitol Complex, 101 S. Fall St., Carson City, NV 89710

State Bureau of Vital Statistics   **702-885-4480**
Dept. of Health, 505 E. King St., Carson City, NV 89710-4761

State Historical Society   **702-789-0190**
1650 N. Virginia St., Reno, NV 89503

Elko County Library   **702-738-3066/N.E. Regional Resource Ctr.: 3077**
720 Court St., Elko, NV 89801

Bureau of Land Management   **702-328-6202**
850 Harvard Way/P.O. Box 1200, Reno, NV 89520

Bar Association   **702-329-4100**
295 Holcomb Ave., Suite 2, Reno, NV 89502-1085

New Hampshire   (records begin approximately 1620)

State Library   **603-271-2394**
20 Park St., Concord, NH 03301

State Law Library   **603-271-3777**
Supreme Court Bldg., 1 Noble Dr., Concord, NH 03301

State Records Management and Archives   **603-271-2236**
71 S. Fruit St., Concord, NH 03301

State Bureau of Vital Statistics   **603-271-4654**
Health and Welfare Bldg., 6 Hazen Dr., Concord, NH 03301-6527

Historical Society   **603-225-3381**
30 Park St., Concord, NH 03301

Bar Association   **603-224-6942**
18 Centre St., Concord, NH 03301

New Jersey (records begin approximately 1609)

State Archives and Library   **609-292-6200/archives: 530-3200**
185 W. State St., Trenton, NJ 08625

State Bureau of Vital Records   **609-292-4087**
Dept. of Health, CN 360, Trenton, NJ 08625-0360

State Historical Society   **201-483-3939**
230 Broadway, Newark, NJ 07104

Federal Archives and Records Center   **201-823-7252**
Bldg. No. 22, Military Ocean Terminal, Bayonne, NJ 07002-5388

Sons of the American Revolution   **201-467-1771**
P.O. Box 168, Springfield, NJ 07081

State Dept. of Law   **609-292-4958**
CN 115 Hughes Justice Complex, Trenton, NJ 08625

Rutgers University   **201-932-7505**
Alexander Library, New Brunswick, NJ 08903

Bar Association   **201-249-5000**
1 Constitution Square (Ryders Lane), New Brunswick, NJ 08901-1500

New Mexico (records begin approximately 1854)

State Library   **505-827-3800/law: 3830**
325 Don Gaspar Ave., Santa Fe, NM 87503

State Archives   **505-827-8860**
404 Montezuma, Santa Fe, NM 87503

State Vital Records Office   **505-827-2338**
Health Services Division, P.O. Box 968, Santa Fe, NM 87504-0968

U.S. Bureau of Land Management   **505-988-6530**
Box 1449, Santa Fe, NM 87504

Special Collections Library   **505-848-1376**
423 Central Ave., N.E., Albuquerque, NM 87102

University of New Mexico   **505-277-4241**
Albuquerque, NM 87131

State Museum History Library   **505-827-6470**
110 Washington Ave./P.O. Box 2087, Santa Fe, NM 87504

Historical Society   **505-277-5839**
Box 4638, Santa Fe, NM 87501

Bar Association   **505-842-6132**
1117 Stanford Dr., N.E., Albuquerque, NM 87130

New York (records begin approximately 1630)

State Archives and Library   **518-474-1195/5930**
Cultural Education Center, Empire State Plaza, Albany, NY 12230

State Law Library   **518-474-3840**
The Capitol, Albany, NY 12224

New York Historical Society 212-873-3400
170 Central Park W., New York, NY 10024

New York Public Library 212-930-0828/0800
5th Ave. and 42nd St., New York, NY 10018

New York Genealogical and Biographical Society 212-755-8532
122 E. 58th St., New York, NY 10022

Brooklyn Historical Society 718-624-0890
128 Pierrepont St., Brooklyn, NY 11201

Municipal Archives (NY City) 212-566-5292/4285
31 Chambers St., New York, NY 10007

Roswell Flower Memorial Genealogical Library 315-788-2352
229 Washington St., Watertown, NY 13601

State Health Department (vital records NY State) 518-474-2121/6172
Empire State Plaza, Wadsworth Center, Albany, NY 12201

Bureau of Vital Statistics (NY City) 212-619-4530
125 Worth St., New York, NY 10013

Schomburg Research Center for Black Culture 212-862-4000
515 Malcolm X Blvd., New York, NY 10037

Albany Institute of History and Art 518-463-4478
125 Washington Ave., Albany, NY 12210

Huguenot Society 212-755-0592
122 E. 58th St., New York, NY 10022

American Irish Historical Society 212-288-2263
991 5th Ave., New York, NY 10028

Yivo Institute for Jewish Research 212-535-6700
1048 5th Ave., New York, NY 10028

The Holland Society of New York 212-758-1675
122 E. 58th St., New York, NY 10022

Bar Association 518-463-3200
One Elk St., Albany, NY 12207

North Carolina   (records begin approximately 1663)

State Library and Archives 919-733-3270/archives: 7305
109 E. Jones St., Raleigh, NC 27611

State Highway Department Survey Unit 919-250-4109
1020 Birch Ridge Dr., Raleigh, NC 27610

State Birth and Death Records 919-733-3526
225 N. McDowell St., P.O. Box 2091, Raleigh, NC 27602

State Marriage and Divorce Records 919-733-3000
225 N. McDowell St., P.O. Box 2091, Raleigh, NC 27602

Supreme Court Library 919-733-3425
2 E. Morgan St./P.O. Box 28006, Raleigh, NC 27611

Historic Foundation of Presbyterians 704-669-7061
318 Georgia Terrace/P.O. Box 847, Montreat, NC 28757

Bar Association   **919-828-4620**
208 Fayetteville Street Mall, Raleigh, NC 27611

North Dakota   (records begin approximately 1870)

State Law Library   **701-224-2221**
Supreme Court, State Capitol Bldg., Bismarck, ND 58505

State Archives and Historical Research Library   **701-224-2668/2490**
Liberty Memorial Bldg., Bismarck, ND 58505

State Vital Records   **701-224-2360**
Dept. of Health, Statistical Service, State Capitol, Bismarck, ND 58505

State Historical Society   **701-224-2666**
Liberty Memorial Bldg., Bismarck, ND 58505

Minot Public Library   **701-852-1045**
516 2nd Ave., S.W., Minot, ND 58701

Bar Association   **701-255-1404**
515½ E. Broadway, Suite 101, Bismarck, ND 58501

Ohio   (records begin approximately 1783)

State Library   **614-644-7061**
65 S. Front St., Rm. 1206, Columbus, OH 43266

State Archives and Documents   **614-466-1500**
1985 Velma Ave., Columbus, OH 43211

State Bureau of Vital Statistics   **614-466-2566**
Health Dept., Rm. G-20, Ohio Depts. Bldg., 65 S. Front St.,
Columbus, OH 43215

State Historical Society   **614-297-2300/2510**
1985 Velma Ave., Columbus, OH 43211

Cleveland Public Library   **216-623-2800**
325 Superior Ave., Cleveland, OH 44114

Case Western Reserve (Freiberger) Library   **216-368-3530/3506**
11161 East Blvd., Cleveland, OH 44106

Online Computer Library Center   **614-764-6000**
6565 Frantz Rd., Dublin, OH 43017

Ohioana Library   **614-466-3831**
1105 Ohio Depts. Bldg., 65 S. Front St., Columbus, OH 43266

Bar Association   **614-421-2121**
33 W. 11th, Columbus, OH 43201

Oklahoma   (records begin approximately 1866)

Division of Archives and Records   **405-521-2502**
200 N.E. 18th St., Oklahoma City, OK 73105

Law Library   **405-278-1353**
321 Park Ave., Rm. 247, Oklahoma City, OK 73102

Choctaw Nation Library System   **918-426-0456**
401 N. 2nd Ave., McAlester, OK 74501

State General Information   405-521-2011
  6601 N. Broadway Ext., Oklahoma City, OK 73116

State Bureau of Vital Statistics   405-271-4040
  Dept. of Health, P.O. Box 53551, Oklahoma City, OK 73152-3551

State Historical Society   405-521-2491
  2100 N. Lincoln Blvd., Oklahoma City, OK 73105

Tulsa Library   918-596-7977
  400 Civic Center, Tulsa, OK 74103

Cherokee Nation Historical Society   918-456-5511
  Box 515, Tahlequah, OK 74465

Bar Association   405-524-2365
  1901 N. Lincoln Blvd., Oklahoma City, OK 73105

Oregon   (records begin approximately 1851)
State Library   503-378-4277/4243
  Summer and Court Sts., N.E., Salem, OR 97310

State Division of Archives   503-378-4241
  1005 Broadway, N.E., Salem, OR 97310

State Bureau of Vital Statistics   503-229-5710
  1400 S.W. 5th Ave./P.O. Box 116, Portland, OR 97207-0116

State Historical Society   503-222-1741
  1230 S.W. Park Ave., Portland, OR 97205

Portland Genealogical Forum   503-227-2398
  Neighbors of Woodcraft Bldg., 1410 S.W. Morrison,
  Portland, OR 97205

Supreme Court Library   503-378-6030
  Supreme Court Bldg., Salem, OR 97310

Bureau of Land Management   503-231-6274
  825 Mutnomah St./P.O. Box 2965, Portland, OR 97208

Bar Association   503-620-0222
  5200 S.W. Meadows Rd./P.O. Box 1689, Lake Oswego, OR 97035

Pennsylvania   (records begin approximately 1681)
State Archives   717-787-3051
  Third and Foster Sts., P.O. Box 1026, Harrisburg, PA 17120

State Library   717-787-2646/law: 3273
  Walnut and Commonwealth Sts., P.O. Box 1601,
  Harrisburg, PA 17105

Federal Archives and Records Center   215-951-5588
  5000 Wissahickon Ave., Philadelphia, PA 19144

Philadelphia City Register (archives)   215-686-6285
  340 S. 11th St., 6th Floor, Philadelphia, PA 19107

Free Library of Philadelphia   215-686-5322
  Logan Square, Philadelphia, PA 19103

State Division of Vital Records **412-656-3126**
Dept. of Health, Central Bldg., P.O. Box 1528, New Castle, PA 16103

Genealogical Society of Pennsylvania/ **215-545-0391/**
Historical Society of Pennsylvania **732-6200**
1300 Locust St., Philadelphia, PA 19107

Historical Commission **717-783-9898**
Third and North Sts./P.O. Box 1026, Harrisburg, PA 17120

Historical Society of Western Pennsylvania **412-681-5533**
4338 Bigelow Blvd., Pittsburgh, PA 15213

Balch Institute **215-925-8090**
18 S. 7th St., Philadelphia, PA 19106

Germantown Historical Society **215-844-0514**
5503 Germantown Ave., Philadelphia, PA 19144

Bar Association **717-238-6715**
100 South St./P.O. Box 186, Harrisburg, PA 17108

Rhode Island (records begin approximately 1648)

State Law Library **401-277-3275**
250 Benefit St., Providence, RI 02903

State Archives **401-277-2353**
State Capitol, Rm. 43, Providence, RI 02903

Providence Athenaeum **401-421-6970**
215 Benefit St., Providence, RI 02903

State Division of Vital Statistics **401-277-2812**
Health Dept., Cannon Bldg., Rm. 101, 75 Davis St.,
Providence, RI 02908

Historical Society **401-331-8575**
121 Hope St., Providence, RI 02906

Providence Public Library **401-455-8000**
225 Washington St., Providence, RI 02903

John Carter Brown Library **401-863-2725/2167**
Brown University, Box 1894, Providence, RI 02912

Bar Association **401-421-5740**
91 Friendship St., Providence, RI 02903

South Carolina (records begin approximately 1670)

State Library **803-734-8666**
1500 Senate St., P.O. Box 11469, Columbia, SC 29211

Department of Archives and History **803-734-8577**
1430 Senate St., Box 11669, Columbia, SC 29211

State Bureau of Vital Statistics **803-734-4830**
Dept. of Health, 2600 Bull St., Columbia, SC 29201

Historic Columbia Foundation **803-252-7742**
1601 Richland St., Columbia, SC 29201

South Carolina Library, Thomas Cooper Library   803-777-4866/3142
University of South Carolina, Columbia, SC 29201

Historical Society   803-723-3225
100 Meeting St., Charleston, SC 29401

Bar Association   803-799-6653
950 Taylor St./Box 608, Columbia, SC 29202

South Dakota   (records begin approximately 1855)

State Library   605-773-3131
800 Governors Dr., Pierre, SD 57501

State Archives   605-773-3804
East Highway Bypass, Pierre, SD 57501

State Bureau of Public Statistics   605-773-3355
Dept. of Health, Joe Foss Office Bldg., 523 E. Capitol,
Pierre, SD 57501

Law Library   605-773-4898
500 E. Capitol Ave., Pierre, SD 57501

Bureau of Indian Affairs   605-473-5510
Brule Sioux High School/P.O. Box 245, Lower Brule, SD 57548

State Historical Society   605-773-3458
Capitol Bldg., 900 Governors Dr., Pierre, SD 57501

Bar Association   605-224-7554
222 E. Capitol, Pierre, SD 57501

Tennessee   (records begin approximately 1778)

State Law Library (Supreme Court)   615-741-2016
401 7th Ave. N., Nashville, TN 37219-0609

State Library and Archives   615-741-2451/2764
403 7th Ave. N., Nashville, TN 37219

Chattanooga, Hamilton Co. Bicentennial Library   615-757-5310
1001 Broad St., Chattanooga, TN 37402

State Vital Records Department   615-741-1763
Cordell Hull Bldg., Nashville, TN 37219

Historical Society   615-242-1796
300 Capitol Blvd., Nashville, TN 37243

Bar Association   615-383-7421
3622 West End Ave., Nashville, TN 37205

Texas   (records begin approximately 1519)

State Library   512-463-5455/archives: 5480
1201 Brazos/P.O. Box 12927, Austin, TX 78711

Federal Archives and Records Center   817-334-5525
501 W. Felix St./Box 6216, Fort Worth, TX 76115

State Bureau of Vital Statistics   512-458-7111
Dept. of Health, 1100 W. 49th St., Austin, TX 78756

Historical Society (Episcopal)   **512-472-6816**
606 Rathervue Place, Austin, TX 78705

Fort Worth Public Library   **817-870-7700**
300 Taylor St., Fort Worth, TX 76102

Houston Public Library   **713-236-1313**
500 McKinney Ave., Houston, TX 77002

Dallas Public Library   **214-670-1400**
1515 Young St., Dallas, TX 75201

Genealogical Research Library   **214-670-1433**
4524 Edmundson Ave., Dallas, TX 75201

Amarillo Genealogical Library   **806-378-3054**
Box 2171, Amarillo, TX 79189

Law Library   **512-463-1722**
121 W. 14th St., Austin, TX 78711

Bar Association   **512-463-1463**
1414 Colorado/P.O. Box 12487, Austin, TX 78711

Utah   (records begin approximately 1847)

State Library   **801-466-5888/law: 538-1045**
2150 S. 300 West, Suite 16, Salt Lake City, UT 84115

State Archives   **801-538-3012**
Archives Bldg., State Capitol, Rm. 28, Salt Lake City, UT 84114

State Bureau of Vital Statistics   **801-538-6105**
288 N. 1460 West/P.O. Box 16700, Salt Lake City, UT 84116

Family History Library   **801-240-2531**
35 N. West Temple, Salt Lake City, UT 84150

Genealogical Society Library   **801-240-2331**
50 E. North Temple, Salt Lake City, UT 84150

State Historical Society   **801-533-5755/5808**
300 Rio Grande, Salt Lake City, UT 84101

Genealogical Helper Library   **801-752-6022**
Everton Publishers, 3223 S. Main St., Nibley, UT 84321

American Genealogical Lending Library   **801-298-5358**
593 W. 100 North/P.O. Box 244, Bountiful, UT 84011

Genealogical and Microforms Library   **801-378-6200**
Harold Lee Library, Brigham Young University, Provo, UT 84602

Association of Professional Genealogists   **801-364-6269**
P.O. Box 11601, Salt Lake City, UT 84147

U. S. Bureau of Land Management   **801-539-4021**
324 S. State St., Suite 301, Salt Lake City, UT 84111

Bar Association   **801-531-9077**
645 S. 200 East, Salt Lake City, UT 84111

Vermont   (records begin approximately 1688)

Department of Libraries   802-828-3261
109 State St., 1st Floor, Montpelier, VT 05602

State Archives   802-828-2308/2363
Redstone Bldg., 26 Terrace St., Montpelier, VT 05602

State Public Records Division   802-828-3286
133 State St., Montpelier, VT 05602

State Vital Records Unit   802-863-7275
60 Main St./P.O. Box 70, Burlington, VT 05402

State Historical Society   802-828-2291
109 State St., Pavilion Bldg., Montpelier, VT 05602

Genealogical Library   802-447-1571
Bennington Museum, Bennington, VT 05201

Chittenden County Law Library   802-863-3403
235 College St., Burlington, VT 05401

Bar Association   802-223-2020
35 Court St., Montpelier, VT 05602

Virginia   (records begin approximately 1607)

State Library   804-786-2332/archives: 2306
11th and Capitol Sts., Richmond, VA 23219

State Division of Vital Records   804-780-4238
Dept. of Health, James Madison Bldg., Box 1000,
Richmond, VA 23208

Historical Society   804-358-4901
428 N. Blvd., P.O. Box 7311, Richmond, VA 23221

U. S. Geological Survey   703-648-4000/4302
12201 Sunrise Valley Dr., Reston, VA 22092

U. S. Bureau of Land Management (Eastern States)   703-461-1369/1480
350 S. Pickett St., Alexandria, VA 22304

National Genealogical Society Library   703-525-0050
4527 17th St., N., Arlington, VA 22207

Supreme Court Library   804-786-2075
100 N. Ninth St., Richmond, VA 23219

Bar Association   804-786-2061
801 E. Main St., Suite 1000, Ross Bldg., Richmond, VA 23219

Washington   (records begin approximately 1851)

State Law Library   206-357-2136
Temple of Justice Bldg., Olympia, WA 98504

State Archives   206-753-5485
12th and Washington, Olympia, WA 98504

Federal Archives and Records Center   206-526-6501/6507
6125 Sand Point Way, N.E., Seattle, WA 98115

State Bureau of Vital Records   **800-551-0562**
P.O. Box 9709, ET-11, Olympia, WA 98504

State Historical Society   **206-593-2830**
315 N. Stadium Way, Tacoma, WA 98403

Seattle Public Library   **206-386-4636/4100**
1000 Fourth Ave., Seattle, WA 98104

Seattle Genealogical Society   **206-682-1410**
1405 Fifth St./P.O. Box 1708, Seattle, WA 98111

Eastern Washington Historical Society   **509-456-3931**
W. 2316 First Ave., Spokane, WA 99204

Bar Association   **206-448-0441**
500 Westin Bldg., 2001 6th Ave., Seattle, WA 98121

West Virginia (records begin approximately 1748)
State Library   **304-348-2041/law: 2607**
State Capitol, Charleston, WV 25305

State Archives   **304-348-0230**
Capitol Complex, Cultural Center, Charleston, WV 25305

State Division of Vital Statistics   **304-348-2931**
Health Department, State Office Bldg. No. 3, Charleston, WV 25305

Historical Society   **304-348-2278**
Science and Cultural Center, Charleston, WV 25305

Supreme Court Library   **304-348-2607**
Capitol Bldg., Rm. E-404, Charleston, WV 25305

Bar Association   **304-346-8414**
State Capitol, E-400, Charleston, WV 25305

Wisconsin (records begin approximately 1831)
State Library   **608-266-2205/law: 1600**
125 S. Webster St., Madison, WI 53707

State Archives   **608-262-3338**
816 State St., Madison, WI 53706

State Vital Records   **608-266-1371**
Health Department, P.O. Box 309, Madison, WI 53701

State Historical Society   **608-262-3266/3421**
816 State St., Madison, WI 53706

Bar Association   **608-257-3838**
402 W. Wilson, Madison, WI 53703

Wyoming (records begin approximately 1855)
State Library   **307-777-7281/law: 7509**
2301 Capitol Ave., Cheyenne, WY 82002

State Archives and Historical Department   **307-777-7518**
Barrett Bldg., Cheyenne, WY 82002

Vital Records Services   **307-777-7591**
Health and Medical Services, Hathaway Bldg., Cheyenne, WY 82002

U. S. Bureau of Land Management   **307-772-2111**
2515 Warren Ave., P.O. Box 1828, Cheyenne, WY 82003

Bar Association   **307-632-9061**
500 Randall Ave., Cheyenne, WY 82001

Appendix 11

Federal Archives and Records Centers (FARC)
Branch Offices and the Areas They Serve

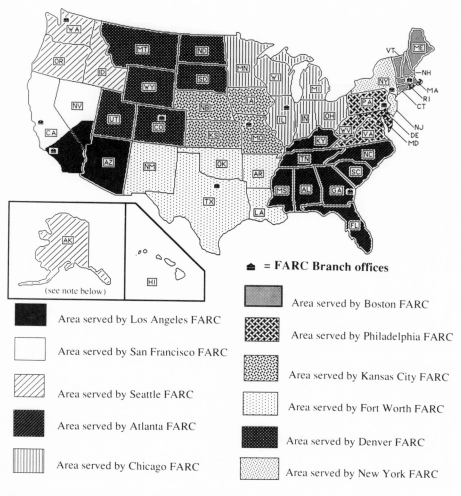

= FARC Branch offices

Area served by Los Angeles FARC

Area served by San Francisco FARC

Area served by Seattle FARC

Area served by Atlanta FARC

Area served by Chicago FARC

Area served by Boston FARC

Area served by Philadelphia FARC

Area served by Kansas City FARC

Area served by Fort Worth FARC

Area served by Denver FARC

Area served by New York FARC

Note: Alaska now has its own FARC and is no longer served by Seattle.

Appendix 12

GENERALIZED RULES OF DESCENT
LAND FLOW MODEL

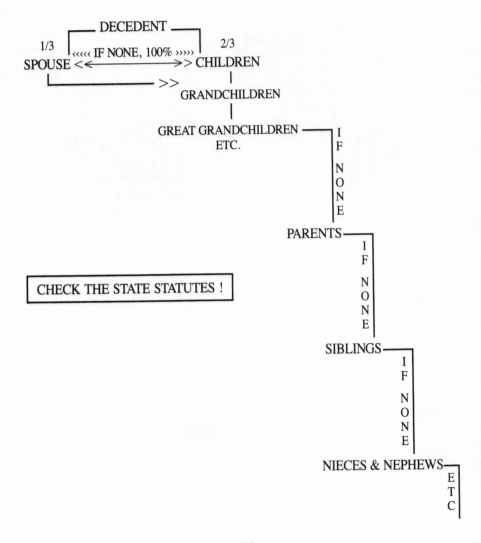

CHECK THE STATE STATUTES !

Acknowledgments

My special thanks to: Terri Taylor for holding me in a higher place that I might discover peace and prosperity; John Adams for the "proper form" and numerous esoteric conversations; Albion Boxill for believing in me; Paul Cotton for the "dis"encouragement, then taking the ball and running with it; Wayne Allinson for all the "technical stuff"; Martha Kudravetz, Ros Harrison, and Jane Douglas (my three island mothers) for their care, concern, faith, and love; Jim Smith for indulging a friend and novice in the face of "The Law"; John Campbell for listening and computing (you are my ever-present beacon); Peggy O'Neil and her powerful, committed heart (I wrote till I was complete, in silence, with eyes cast down); Razz Ingrasci (you really showed up); Jim McCann (we've come a long way, buddy); Kathy Timledge (the nice one); Chris Lee; Dorothy Hay (I love my senior, I love my senior); Barbara (Robo) Roberto (or was that Dorothy Roberto and Barbara Hay); Lisa Monaco (thanks for the unconditionality); Adam Weiner for tons of support; Michael Sugarman for "springer guidance"; George Crotty and everyone else in Lifespring for "who they were in the matter" that this wicked promoter actually finished something (I'm It); Allan Weiner, Annette Pingry, Suzanne Gauger, Andrew Steele, Revolution #9, LP 29 & 31, for their hearts, feedback, and "unreasonable" support (you guys really showed up for me); Midge(y) Silvio for the beauty of transformation; Kathy McEniff for her powerful inspiration; Stuart Abrams, Robbie Bridgewater, and Liz Lewis for their friendship, risking "input" and "legalese"; Florence, Pam, Diana, and Peter for their patience, honesty, and authenticity; George, Val, and Linda for listening and responding authentically, logically, and diplomatically; Cheryl Aldwardt for her kindness and understanding; the rest of the registry regulars for assisting a "helpless male"; everyone at the Historical Society, especially Kay and Leanne for proving that perseverance is the key; Tom Emerson for showing that each person is a new opportunity; Mike McLaughlin for camaraderie, laughs and talks; and soldiers Joyce, Martha, Ros, Dave, and Don for proofreading. Special editorial thanks to Michael, Joe, Stu, and Rachael (the grammar police); to Eileen, Julie, Ed, and Denise for design; to Harry and Phene for typesetting; my family and friends for "being there"; Mom and Dad for that innate "Segel Drive"; and lastly, and, once again, to my wife Shelly, my son Kevin, and the others who may follow, thank you for everything.

This book remembers Jack Sullivan and Ben Harrison
for their spirit, peace, support, friendship, and love.

Index